“DEMONS
OR
ANGELS”

BONNIE B. BELL

BALBOA.PRESS
A DIVISION OF HAY HOUSE

Balboa Press books may be ordered through booksellers or by contacting:

Balboa Press
A Division of Hay House
1663 Liberty Drive
Bloomington, IN 47403
www.balboapress.com
844-682-1282

Print information available on the last page.

ISBN: 978-1-9822-5782-8 (sc)
ISBN: 978-1-9822-5794-1 (e)

Balboa Press rev. date: 11/18/2020

CONTENTS

PREFACE

I started writing this over forty years ago after I witnessed an unidentified flying object. It was early morning, and a UFO was hovering in the sky over a military base. The guard spotted it first and said, "Oh My God, a UFO." Looking up, you could see it was round, silver in color, and there was no mistaking what it was.

I heard during that time; Christ was going to return. Some Bible scholars proclaim unidentified flying objects are in the Bible because Ezekiel saw a whirlwind come out of the sky. This story is in Ezekiel, chapter one. Although this book doesn't explore this hypothesis, it made me realize there is more to life than we know.

Growing up, I was given moral standards as a compass; yet, my peers had failed me, and I suffered many things. I came to the realization and witnessed people were mainly out for themselves. Not wanting this type of life, I decided to seek the truth, picked up a Bible, a Bible concordance, a dictionary, and began my studies.

During those days, I was on Guam, which is an island in the Pacific Ocean. And I understood by Scripture the Lord told us to seek him and to pray in private. I genuinely believe in the Lord. Not only in the air but an actual person that lives in heaven. I would sit on the beach and look for him to come from heaven to help me. I'd been in hell all my life, so I sure didn't want to go to a worse place when I died.

After many days I was enlightened by an incredible experience, not of this world. Scripture tells us he would do a work in our day that people would not believe. This quote is found in Habakkuk chapter one, verse five. So, I won't go into what it was I experienced here.

In my excitement, I went to the religions and explained what had happened. Of course, the Jewish and various Christian beliefs are supposed to preach the Old and New Testament of the Bible. So, I went to them, assuming they would understand. Instead, the incident I had experienced wasn't anything they teach.

However, the experience I had was what Christ taught, so was I going to believe how they interpreted this portion of the Bible or what happened? Rejected, I went on a one-person mission to find the truth.

I even traveled from one end of the world to the other, but what I found was all nations had adopted the God of their peers; if it is a form of Christianity, Jewish, Buddhist, or Muslim. So, all peoples are like sheep and follow their fathers' teachings without questioning.

To my amazement, I found those who claim to base their beliefs on the Bible teach many contradictions. Because you can give a verse to different people and get other translations, yet they all hold to the fact Scripture was inspired by one author, and that is the Holy Spirit. They all claim to have the Holy Spirit within them, and it is he that wrote Scripture yet cannot interpret it the same way? As the author of what He wrote doesn't know what He meant?

On top of all that, I found cults like Heaven's Gate, who believed in UFOs and God. Were they telling us the truth, or does the Word of God testify against them? This book is not how I judge anyone. I will explain what the Bible says, but it is the Word of God that shall judge all.

As Christ told us in the last days, many ***false prophets*** would deceive many, because people would love sin, and their love for the Lord would wax cold. As Mathew twenty-four, verse eleven, states: they would acknowledge and say Jesus is the Christ, yet deny his teachings.

Furthermore, Scripture reveals in second Corinthians eleven, verse four, the reason this is happening is that two thousand years ago, there were impostors who had abandoned the truth by ***preaching another Jesus*** or savior. These imposters would be made known at the end of days and are like a prostitute who would sell their faith for money. They would have many confusing mixed up teachings and are referred to as Babylon in Revelation. Babylon in Scripture was a city that was confused and mixed up in speech, while these have contradicting theology.

My goal is to prove to you; the Bible is true, as I know beyond a doubt, men directed by the Holy Spirit wrote the Bible. And because God is all-powerful and omnipotent in that he created the world and everything in it. Plus, He is the Word, whereby it was not a difficult task for him to keep His Bible intact. Thereby, the Bible does not lie, and Scripture cannot say one thing in one place and meaning something else in another section for God is not a hypocrite.

CHAPTER 1

The Beginning

Adam and Eve

In the first chapter of Revelation, we found Christ is the beginning and the end. And for this reason, we will look at the beginning and how creation came about.

When you read Genesis, at first, it seems like Adam and Eve were the only two people God created, and that is usually how the story goes. Yet, upon an additional study of the Bible, you'll find other people existed too. And the first question people have is, "Where did these people come from?"

Many speculate the reason there were other human beings, but when you search Scripture you will find the reason explained in Genesis five, verse two. That tells us when God created human beings: ***male and female created them. and blessed them, and called their name Adam, in the day when they were created, Gn 5:2.*** In other words, what that explains is, the first men and women established were named Adam. The name Adam in Hebrew translated means human being.

Additionally, Scripture explains when God created humankind, He said to those in heaven, ***"Let's make man in our image"***. That is in Genesis one, verse twenty-six. So, to whom was the Lord-God speaking? It was the angels in heaven, as many scriptures tell us they resemble humankind. Thereby, the angels are the ***men of heaven***, as even Revelation five, verse three suggests.

Then when the ***Lord God planted a garden eastward in Eden there, He put the man whom He had formed, Gn 2:8.*** The Adam in the Garden had his job to dress and keep the Garden as Genesis two: fifteen explains.

Whereas, those who were created by those in heaven were scattered outside of the Garden. Their job was to, ***"have dominion over the fish of the sea, and over the fowl of the air, and over the cattle, and overall the earth, and over every creeping thing that creepeth upon the earth" Gn 2:26.***

The Lord choosing Adam in the Garden of Eden is not to say others created were inferior, but the Lord-God has always had those he elected, like Abraham, Moses, or Lot. Even Christ explained, ***"Many are called but few chosen,"*** written in Matthew seven, verse thirteen. As Christ also warned, it would be ***"A narrow gate"*** and not the wide gate many claims are available. All testified in Matthew twenty-two, verse fourteen.

Thereby, the Lord chose the man He created and placed him in the Garden. He told Adam: ***"Of every tree of the garden thou may eat. But of the tree of knowledge of good and evil, you shalt not eat of it: for in the day that thou eats thereof you shall surely die" Gn 2:15-17.*** And that is written in the King James Bible.

Adam and Eve residing in the Garden of Eden, a serpent approached Eve and convinced ***her she would not surely die;*** recorded in Genesis three verse four. Did a snake talk? It's not how the serpent conveyed his message. But what I do know, as an example, my dog lets me know when she wants to go outside, when she wants to go to bed, and if she wants a treat.

Nonetheless, Jeremiah seventeen verse nine explains ***the heart is deceitful and WHO can know it? I the Lord search the heart, I try the reins, even to give every man according to his ways, and according to the fruit of his doings Jer 17:9.*** What that says is God gave us two eyes to see, ears to hear, a mouth to talk, and a mind to think. But what motivates an individual given a free will could not be determined. Thereby, when the Lord God created humankind, everyone's motives had to be tested. Having to try humanity was the apparent reason the forbidden tree of knowledge was even in the Garden.

So regardless of how the serpent communicated his message, what is essential to understand is Eve didn't believe what the Lord instructed; rather, she decided to accept the lies the snake shared. Hence, she ate the fruit and also convinced Adam to eat some.

The next thing I realized is God does not use our standard of time. Scripture explains a thousand years, to God, is like one day. Scripture also explains: all the days that Adam lived *were nine hundred and thirty years*: and he died. If God is true and he told Adam he would die the same day he ate the fruit. Therefore, Adam died before he was a thousand years old, which was in God's time. All written in Second Peter three: eight, Genesis five: five, Genesis three: twenty-two.

Although Scripture also explains a person who is seeking self-gratification can be dead even while they are alive. And that can be found in first Timothy five, verse six. And because God cannot lie, we know, either way, in the day Adam and Eve ate of this fruit, their fate sealed, and they died.

Before Adam and Eve passed away, they had two sons named Cain and the other Able. We don't know how all of the circumstances unfolded. But what is known is Cain was jealous of Able, and he killed his brother, Genesis four.

After Cain killed his brother, the Lord appeared unto Cain and asked him what he had done. Of course, the Lord was aware Cain had killed his brother and having no remorse, Cain asked the Lord, ***"Am I my brother's keeper? Gn 4:9"*** So, when the Lord passed judgment upon Cain, He told Cain he would be cast out of his presence and ordered out of the Garden of Eden. Again, written in Genesis four.

Being commissioned out of the Garden, Cain was fearful for his life, as he knew those who lived outside of the Garden of Eden would want to kill him. And the reason Cain was afraid was that he realized his family, when chosen, were put in ***the Garden to dress it and to keep it, Gn 2:15—written*** in King James Bible. Dressing the Garden meant they were the Garden's caretakers. At one time, they provided the fruit of the Garden to all. However, once Adam disobeyed the Lord, and the tree of life was abolished. Not having this fruit available resulted in all dying. This caused all who lived outside of the Garden of Eden to blame Adam's family.

Additionally, because thorns and weeds started growing and the eatable fruit was not as plenteous. Men were dying, and it was hard to develop a garden which caused the children of men to blame God's children for their demise. Cain, knowing this, realized being thrown out of the presence of the Lord, he would not have the same protection and knew if they recognized him, they would want to kill him.

Therefore, Cain pleaded for his life, explained to the Lord if the Lord cast him out of his presence, the nation's people would want to kill him. And because judgment belongs to the Lord God, He granted Cain's life to be prolonged. For you see, God is good; whereby our Lord helps all and even causes the sun to rise and set on the good and evil—***written*** in Matthew five: forty-five. So, when the Lord sent Cain out of his presence, He disguised Cain so others would not recognize him. These stories can be found in Matthew seven verses one through three, Psalms seven, verse eight, Matthew five, verse forty-five, and Genesis four, verse fifteen.

Upon leaving the Garden of Eden, Cain traveled to Nod, where he met his wife, Genesis four. How far Cain had to travel to get to Nod is unclear, but I doubt it was too far perhaps only a day's journey. When created, People generally lived in the same area. I'm not sure of any transportation mode, but I suspect they may have used horses, camels, or mules. Yet, generally speaking, we know all human life when created was on the same continent.

It is also unclear what type of animals lived in the same general vicinity as human-beings, due to the fact. Adam named the animals that were brought to him by the Lord, Genesis two, verse nineteen. I have to presume the larger or fiercer beasts were relocated to another continent after Adam named them. So, on that day, if there had been a map of the known world, it may have looked like just one continent. They probably were not aware of any other continents. Nor did they know about Africa, where the more massive and fiercer animals had been relocated and lived. After all, it was just a little over two hundred years ago, and people still thought the earth was flat.

NOAH

Back then, as the years and generations passed, the population began experiencing many of the same cares and problems in life that we share. The years had passed, and bye and bye, the Garden of Eden eventually faded into a dim memory.

As we see now, back then, violence began to show its ugly head, whereby; lawlessness began to rule. At which point, Scripture tells us ***the sons of God lusted after the daughters of men Gn 6:11***, King James Bible.

What on earth does it mean when Scripture mentions the Sons of God and daughters of men? To understand what that means is when God chose a people, they were heirs of Abraham, making them the sons of God. If you were outside of that clan, you were called a gentile and the son of man.

During the days of Adam and Eve, God sons were a direct ancestor to Adam. Due to this was whom our Lord and God created. Children born outside of the Garden of Eden were considered the children of men. Created by the angels in heaven, the children outside of the Garden were the children of men. The Hebrew language is not like English and when it speaks of men and women it's in a masculine format. Thereby, children of men would apply to both sexes.

In any case, it was in Noah's day, and, like now, there was looting, rioting, and killing going on.

Furthermore, when God established the Garden of Eden, the Lord provided Adam with one wife, Eve. The decedents of Adam and Eve slept around and took as many wives as they wanted. And sexual immorality became unobstructed, which grieved the Lord God. So, when God saw the ancestors of Adam and Eve corrupting their ways, the Lord said, "***The wickedness of man was great in the***

earth. My spirit shall not always strive with man for that he also flesh." And it repented the Lord that he had made man on the earth, and it grieved him at his heart Gn 6:1-7. All reported in Genesis six, verses one through seven in the King James Bible.

However, during those days, ***there was a man named Noah and he found grace in the eyes of the Lord Gn 6:8.*** And the Lord said unto Noah, "***The end of all flesh has come before me; for the earth is filled with violence through them, and behold, I will destroy them with the earth. Make thee an ark of gopher wood; rooms shalt thou make in the Ark, and shalt pitch it within and without with pitch Gn 6:13-14"***, King James Bible.

Noah believed what the Lord God said and did accordingly, and it is my understanding, the Ark was approximately 450 feet long and 75 feet wide, and 45 feet high. To put this in perspective, an Ark, the size of a football field? When a football field is 360 feet long, and 160 feet wide seems a bit small.

Aboard the Ark, food had to last forty days, and what animals lived on the landmass where Noah and all people lived, only God knows. And this is another reason I have to believe the larger and more ferocious animals had been relocated to another continent by the Lord after Adam named them. ***Adam naming the animals*** is recorded in Geneses two verse twenty.

Genesis six, verse nineteen, explains how the Lord told Noah, ***"to Take of every living thing of all flesh,***

two of every sort shalt thou bring into the ark, to keep them alive with thee, they shall be male and female." Yet cows, chickens, and animals that were for human consumption; Noah was told to take seven of those Gn 7:2. And that is reported in Genesis seven, verse two in the King James Bible.

Noah had to gather food for both the animals and his family. And the more animals, the more food had to be taken aboard—as it had to last forty days. If there had been carnivore animals, like lions, Noah would have had to have taken even more animals.

Once Noah had finished building the Ark and gathering all the animals, the Lord said unto Noah, ***"Come thou and all thy house into the ark; for thee have I seen righteous before me in this generation Gn 7:1".*** All other people drowned after Noah and his family entered into the Ark.

Of course, we can't be sure what animals were aboard the Ark. Yet, when we look around, we see the difference in our ethnicity. Thereby, we know someone in Noah's family was black, yellow, brown, and white.

Once they departed, the Ark people began to prosper and multiply. After some generations passed, humans began to repopulate the earth. Upon which time, the ancestors of Noah all spoke the same language. Whereby, all ***people were of one language, and of one speech, Gn 11:9.***

BABYLON

Then for reasons unknown, there came a time they decided to venture and travel from the area they populated. We don't know the circumstances or reasons they chose to relocate. But when they moved, they ***journeyed from the east, where they found a plain in the land of Shinar; and they dwelt there,*** **Gn 11:2.**

They had stories of the flood. Yet the descendants of Noah, like in our day, everyone is knowledgeable regarding this cataclysm. Yet, being knowledgeable about something doesn't mean you believe it, in your heart, Romans ten, verse seventeen, and Luke eleven verse twenty-eight.

We can compare it to many in this day who build space ships and fly to heaven in search of other life. Back then, I am sure they were perplexed too and asked themselves; if there is a God who created life, what was the reason, he made only them?

Beginning their journey, the descendants of Noah traveled to a place called Shinar. And because they were confused and somewhat bewildered when they didn't find any other living beings; they decided to leave a footprint and name for themselves. Whence they said, ***"Go to, let us build us a city and a tower, whose top may reach unto heaven; and let us make us a name lest we be scattered abroad upon the face of the whole earth,"*** **Gn 11:3-4.**

Invariably ***the Lord came down to see the city and the tower, which the children of men built. And the Lord***

said to the men of heaven, "Behold, the people is one, and they have all one language, and this they begin to do; and now nothing will be restrained from them Gn 11:5-6." All recorded in Genesis eleven, verses five through seven in the King James Bible. At which time, the Lord continued telling those in the Kingdom of heaven, ***"Let us go down, and there confound their language, that they may not understand one another's speech" Gn 11:7.*** So, from that time on, when those in heaven came down, and by ethnicity, they confounded everyone's language. As exemplified in our day and apparent, yellow people began speaking Japanese, while others started speaking Chinese.

How the Lord-God accomplished this feat is a mystery. But it was at this time, the Lord gave the city a new name Babylon. Yet we know back then, everyone still colonized the same continent, but they could no longer understand each other's speech, and it was, for this reason.

Hence those who spoke English began congregating in one area; those who spoke French assembled elsewhere. Some began speaking Swahili massed in other regions where they could understand each other. Even people who spoke Spanish gathered in a different area, and so forth.

And to keep the children of men from learning each other's language science reveals, great earthquakes, and archaeology digs prove the earth went through some terrible upheavals. This cataclysm was so bad it caused the ground to break apart and separate. Whereby the peoples of this world were scattered abroad upon the face of the earth. They left in ruination and the building of that great city Babylon.

Whereby, the ***children of men to be scattered abroad from thence upon the face of all the earth: and they left off building the city*, *Gn 11:8***.

All cultures know about the flood, but the memory is short. Like those who used to be aware of the Garden of Eden, people no longer spoke of these catastrophes, and everything faded into a distant memory.

But what these stories reveal is we are all from the same family. All of us had an ancestor get off the same boat, being the Ark, regardless of skin color, nationality, where you live in this world, how much money you have, or even how much money you don't have. All of these things have been, and there is nothing new under the sun.

What is vital to see, as it was in the day of Noah so is it now. And, ***when the land sins against the Lord by trespassing grievously, and considers His Word dung; He will stretch out his hand upon it, and will break the staff of the bread thereof. And although Noah, Daniel and Job were in it, as I live, says the Lord God, they shall deliver neither son nor daughter; they shall deliver their own souls by their righteousness Ez 14:14-20.*** To name other chapters this is written, is Ezekiel fourteen, chapter fourteen, Ezekiel fourteen verse twenty, and John twelve, verse forty King James version.

Proverbs twenty chapter five tells us counsel in man's heart is like deep water, but a man of understanding will draw it out.

And what Proverbs means is a man can imagine many things. But a person with understanding will eventually perceive and get it.

So, I hope by the previous chapter, you can see how people will look at the same situation or read the same chapters in the Bible and have different opinions and translations. First Corinthians two, verses ten and eleven, explains this by saying ***a person with the Spirit of God will understand things written in Scripture by the Spirit of God. In contrast, a person without God's Spirit will view things by a man's understanding 1 Co 2:10-11.*** Governed by the flesh, means by their imagination, and not the Spirit of God, whereby a person will perceive many scriptures differently. Causing Scripture to become convoluted because they view things through their heart's desires.

If you have read the King James Bible, I assume you remember the Lord told us ***to take heed how we hear: for whosoever hath, to him shall be given; and whosoever hath not, from him shall be taken even that which he seems to have Lk 8:11.*** The true riches are found in God's word because you are able to understand what He meant. Even Christ said ***to those Jews which believed on him, If ye continue in my word, then are ye my disciples indeed; And ye shall know the truth, and the truth shall make you free Jn 8: 31-32.***

However, when a person is unable to understand what the Lord meant and they are covetous, they assume when Christ said ***whosoever hath, to him shall be given*** this verse means they will get riches and their heart's desires.

Christ gave us a parable in Mark four and Luke eight about a farmer who planted God's Word. The parable explained how some people who heard his words would have little conviction and eventually fall by the wayside. Some may even use his name and appear holy unto others, but in actuality, the love of this world and the deceitfulness of riches would win them over. And like those in Daniel four, ***they praised the gods of gold, silver, brass, iron, wood, and stone,*** thinking this is God's blessings upon them.

Whereby they don't believe Christ's teachings, and to paraphrase what Christ told us in Luke six, verse twenty-four was those who are rich would come into great condemnation. For the riches they received would be their consolation. And at the end of the day, they would weep and howl and find themselves in great distress and discomfort, Jms 5:1. And it's all because they didn't have ears to hear what Christ taught. But were covetous and they nourished their hearts, made them fat, as for a day of slaughter.

And God knows the depths of one's heart by the way we interpret Scripture. And that is the reason I liken the Bible to an inkblot test a Psychiatrist developed, insomuch, by our interpretation it discloses to God Almighty the intent of one's heart. Thereby, those who are covetous will read greed, a lair will not see the truth, ***"but those with an honest and good heart, having heard the Word, keep it, and bring forth fruit with patience. Lk 8:15"***. Therein is the reason you can give Scripture to ten people and get ten different interpretations.

Christ said they teach each other Scripture, and ***in vain they do worship me, teaching for doctrines the commandments of men, Mt 15:9.*** Learning Scripture in this fashion is alarming because if they had received the Spirit that proceeds from God, they would not need teachers as we have a teacher, and that is the Holy Spirit within us. As explained, it is due to ***the anointing which ye have received of him abideth in you, and ye need not that any man teach you: but as the same anointing teacheth you of all things, and is truth, and is no lie, and even as it hath taught you, ye shall abide in him 1 Jn 2:27.***

Taught by the Spirit of God, you would have realized Satan rules in this world, and is referred to as the god of this world in Second Corinthians four, verse four. Even Revelation twelve, verse nine explains how Satan deceives the entire world.

Christ was not Satan's friend. Baptized by John, Christ went out into the wilderness, and the devil tried to trick him. The devil showed Jesus all the world's kingdoms and how they belonged to him. Christ was offered by Satan to be a king over all of the nations. Unlike Adam, who didn't believe God when he was told something, Christ refused. All Recorded in Luke four, verses five through seven.

Satan given the keys to this world, and realizing that you should have known Jesus is our King, President, and Leader. To what do we give allegiance, but heaven as this is our country.

By understanding this world is governed by Satan, why would you want to play a role in politics? The Romans fought for the Roman Empire, but where is the Empire now? The British fought for the British Empire, but where is the British Empire now? The lies, the greed, the hypocrisy in government, and you think this is good?

People say they want to pick the lesser of two evils. We are to flee sin! Not to mention, there was a man who would come and rein by Satan's power and be the epitome of arrogance. He would influence the entire world, but he would especially want to entice Israel. Scripture refers to him as the man of perdition. And this son of hell will be looked at in the next chapter.

What is essential to see is the church began falling away from the truth two thousand years ago.

Paul explained in Acts twenty, verse thirty, and thirty-one that there were imposters dressed in sheep's clothing. Sitting with Paul that day were apostate theologians. He warned how these impostors would not spare the true church. But in fact, they would speak headstrong theology and would be against what Christ taught. Their goal was to make merchandise out of people and to get a following after themselves.

So, I hope you see, because it is one thing to sin which all of us are guilty of, but another thing to be governed by evils depths. One example of a person who is governed by the depths of depravity is those who are serial killers. And if you knew a religious leader was conveying lies to his flock, causing them to die and end up in hell wouldn't you consider this leader a serial killer?

Nonetheless, Solomon explains by the Spirit of God in Proverbs that ***"A wicked doer will give heed to false lips, and a liar will give ear to a mischievous tongue Pr 17:4."*** Telling us, none of us are victims, as we will all be responsible for our actions. Even though Eve blamed the serpent and Adam blamed Eve, they had to take responsibility for their actions.

As for me, I judge no one for it is God who is the Word, and it is Him, I believe, this is what I report, and He is the one who shall judge. For you see, Christ told us in the King James Bible; ***"He that rejects me, and receives not my words, has one that judges him: the word that I have spoken, the same shall judge him in the last day, Jn 12:48."***

CHAPTER 2

Evolution or Revelation

Apostasy

I know evolution makes sense to some people, but then that logic falls apart when you consider the earth, humankind, the animals, and everything you see. All of this happened by accident as some proclaim? Or, like others, profess people are the ancestry of monkeys who evolved and turned into humanity? Even all the DNA ancestry testing in this day has proved this to be a lie.

Yet this book will reveal that we are basically like a species created and exiled to a planet to see what makes us, as individuals tick, and why this had to happen.

The tree of knowledge in Eden, revealed the world became the court to test the heart's motives. Don't you see it? God is God, meaning He is supreme and the head of all authority. The Lord God doesn't play politics. Either you love, believe, and follow His teachings, or you don't. He sent Christ to provide a path for us to pursue and testified; ***"If ye keep my commandments, ye shall abide in my love; even as I have kept my Father's commandments, and abide in his love., Jn 15:10."***

The Lord gave Adam and Eve words to follow as they were commanded not to eat from the forbidden tree of knowledge. Yet, the Lord granted the devil via the serpent to approach Eve, who told Eve they *would be like God* ***and not die Gn 3:4.*** By placing a tree in the garden, it allowed the Most-High a way to test their hearts to see whom they would believe.

Satan tempted Jesus as we, too, are tempted by those who are influenced by Satan. And the question has always been, whom do you believe?

As it was explained two thousand years ago in Second Thessalonians two, verse seven, whereas it states ***the mystery*** of iniquity was already at work". As Paul said, ***For the mystery of iniquity doth already work: only he who now letteth will let, until he be taken out of the way 2 Thes 2:7.*** Lawlessness would abound and they would use Christ in name only. Whereby the apostasy ignores God's commandments promises people heaven telling them they will not die. These are the ones who preach ***another Jesus,*** as Second Corinthians, chapter eleven testified. Additionally, Scripture tells us this movement was allowed to flourish and continue until the end of this world.

So, what should be understood is if anyone is of the truth, the Word of God would not be able to testify against them. For it is the Word Christ gave us that shall judge all. As stated in John twelve: forty-eight. For you see the true church, ***shall not live by bread alone but by every Word of God, Mt 4:4.*** You cannot take a portion of the Scripture you like and use other Scripture for your toilet paper as Adam and Eve did.

Nonetheless, Christ knew the world; for the most part, would not accept his teachings. One day, Christ spoke to many in the synagogue, and when the religious heard what he had to say, they were ***filled with wrath. After which they rose, and thrust him out of the city, and led him unto the brow of the hills of the hill whereon their city was built, that they might cast him down Lk 4.***

On that day, many people were more worried about the deceitfulness of riches, or what you eat, and not what you stand for. Christ explained to flee such things. And told us ***to be of good cheer, if we were of the world, the world would love his own: but because we are not of the world, but he chose us out of the world. Therefore the world hates us Mt 15:9-12."*** Christ said many things that they didn't accept, and once they crucified Christ, they also persecuted those who followed Christ's teachings.

History plus many scriptures testify how in that day those of the faith were held in prison, fed to lions, had their heads cut off, etc. People without conviction began to break down as they didn't want this same thing to happen to them.

While others who sought the affection of people changed Christ's words to say smooth things and the falling away began to raise its ugly head in a mighty way. All testified in Second Peter two. Even in this day, those of apostate beliefs change many translations to say smooth things, and have opened a wide gate. Even though Christ said, ***"strait is the gate, and narrow is the way, which leadeth unto life, and few there be that find it".***

So, moving from the milk of God's Word we will look at the deep things Christ taught; whereby, the apostles were also at times perplexed. In fact, one of the disciples, said unto him, ***"Why speakest thou unto them in parables?"*** Christ answered and said unto them, ***"Because it is given unto you to know the mysteries of the kingdom of heaven, but to them it is not given. For whosoever hath, to him shall be given, and he shall have more abundance: but whosoever hath not, from him shall be taken away even that he hath. Therefore, speak I to them in parables: because they seeing see not; and hearing they hear not, neither do they understand" Mt 13: 10-17.***

And because the falling away from the true faith was in progress when Revelation was penned it too had to be written in parables and in a cryptic fashion, as to hide it from these impostors.

And to enable you to understand the mysteries I am about to reveal, you have to realize God's timetable is not the same as ours. Most prophecy can take years, if not thousands of years, to fulfill. For example, people will read Matthew twenty-four. They think all the forecasts Christ mentioned would take place in a generation when the prophecies would take years to complete. So, what Christ meant was when the last prophecy was fulfilled, it would be the last generation. And the final prophecy to be fulfilled that Christ mentioned was the Bible would be published throughout the world.

If you are able to understand how God's timetable works, I will now reveal what the Spirit says regarding Revelation.

REVELATION

Now Revelation starting at verse thirteen may seem perplexing, but to paraphrase what it forewarns and says: two beasts come to power. The way the story unfolds in Revelation is the first beast will suffer a head wound and appears dead when a second beast emerges on the scene.

The second beast acquires all the first beast's power and helps heal the first beast's head wound, whereby he restores the first beast. At which point, the second beast will make an image of the first beast. He will kill everyone who refuses to worship him or the image. This beast has a number for his name, which is 666.

And on top of all that, Revelation sixteen tells us this beast has seven heads. His seven heads are actually mountains. And a woman is sitting on this creature, which is a great city. This woman's name is Babylon; she is a whore, and is drunk in the blood of saints and the martyrs of Christ.

And if that isn't complicated enough, this beast has ten horns, which are kings or kingdoms that receive power for a short time with this animal. These ten horns will eventually hate the whore being this great city and destroy her.

Furthermore, Revelation explains three leading players are members and, in some fashion, help to make up the beast; the first is the beast itself, then there is the dragon, and the false prophet.

The Beast

Now to explain who the beast is in Revelation; you will have to believe what Jesus revealed and taught when he told us if people are "***Not with him they are against him: and he that gathereth not with him scattereth Lk 11:23.*** In other words, a person using Christ in name only but not following his teachings were capable of casting out unclean spirits. But, ***When the unclean spirit is gone out of a man, he walketh through dry places, seeking rest; and finding none, he saith, I will return unto my house whence I came out. And when he cometh, he findeth it swept and garnished. Then goeth he, and taketh to him seven other spirits more wicked than himself; and they enter in, and dwell there: and the last state of that man is worse than the first Lk 11:23-26.***

Telling us if a person had an unclean spirit in him, but when it exits out of a man, he will walk through places and will seek rest. When this evil spirit can't find rest, he'll return to the person he came out of, and takes with him seven other spirits more wicked than himself; and they enter in, and dwell there: and the last state of that person is worse than before." In other words, evil spirits can occupy humans when they are not following Christ's teachings in truth.

Another example of spirit possession was when, Jesus was in the synagogue. ***And in the synagogue there was a man, which had a spirit of an unclean devil, and cried out with a loud voice, Saying, Let us alone; what have we to do with thee, thou Jesus of Nazareth? art thou come to destroy us? I know thee who thou art; the Holy One of God. And Jesus rebuked him, saying, Hold thy peace, and come out of him. And when the devil had thrown him in the midst, he came out of him, and hurt him not. Lk 4: 33-35.*** Showing us, the devil is an unclean evil spirit.

Later that day, ***when the sun was setting, all they that had any sick with divers diseases brought them unto him; and he laid his hands on every one of them, and healed them. And devils also came out of many, crying out, and saying, Thou art Christ the Son of God. And he rebuking them suffered them not to speak: for they knew that he was Christ, Lk 4: 40-41***

Additionally, written in Matthew eight, Jesus was traveling and went to the countryside called Gergesenes. And two men were standing by some tombs possessed with devils. I'm not sure if they lived in the tombs, but they must have appeared as raving maniacs and frightened people who walked by.

The devil being an evil spirit who resided in these men, knows Jesus is the Son of God, but he will not abide in his Word, so when they saw Christ, they cried out, saying, ***What have we to do with thee, Jesus, thou Son of God? art thou come hither to torment us before the time? And there was a good way off from them an herd of many swine feeding. So, the devils besought him, saying, If thou cast us out, suffer us to go away into the herd of swine. And he said unto them, Go. And when they were come out, they went into the herd of swine: and, behold, the whole herd of swine ran violently down a steep place into the sea, and perished in the waters. And they that kept the sheep fled, and went their ways into the city, and told everything, and what was befallen to the men who had been possessed of the devils Mt 8:29-32.***

Thereby, if you believe in Christ and what he taught, you should have been aware of this evil spirit's existence. And whether you believe in this presentation of the Bible or not, the beast is this evil spirit, and the devil spoken of in Revelation!

I know some will deny what Christ taught, claiming the beast would be a man of sin. Unable to believe Jesus they can't comprehend the creature is a spirit. And in truth a Head of state would be possessed and crowned by this evil spirit like the commander and chief. Satan offered this position to Christ when he took Christ into an ***exceeding high mountain, and showed him all the kingdoms of the world, and the glory of them; And saith unto him, All these things will I give thee, if thou wilt fall and worship me Mt 4:8,9***

Satan cast out of heaven was granted kingship of this world, and of course, Christ declined his offer. But the man of sin to be revealed will not refuse this offer and will be possessed with the evil spirit that started this mess while he was in heaven. And Revelation refers to this man as the dragon. Nonetheless, as Christ professed, ***the violent take it by force, Mt 11:12.***

And if you have been able to understand this so far, you should be able to realize when Christ came, two thousand years ago, the inhabitants of the Roman Empire had accomplished many things. They believed their accomplishments were by their endeavors.

After all, they also helped the poor and even fed the hungry. The Jews and the Roman Empire wouldn't accept that if they didn't follow Christ's teachings; this made them evil and capable of being possessed by an evil spirit.

Yet, since the beginning of time, this evil spirit has been cunning and even hides his existence. And because ***people love the darkness they won't come to the light Jn 3:19.***

Tree of Knowledge

Scripture informs us: ***"we wrestle not against flesh and blood, but against principalities, against powers, against the rulers of the darkness of this world, against spiritual wickedness in high places Eph 6:12"*** Thrown out of heaven Satan has been warring with God by deceiving whom he could. Nonetheless, since the Garden of Eden, Satan still knew God spoke the truth even if he refused to follow it. And when the Lord named a tree knowledge in the Garden of Eden, Satan had to have realized it was capable of providing intelligence. To try and defeat God using humans, he decided he would do this by gaining intelligence via humankind.

Thereby, in Genesis three, when Satan deceived Eve, ***"And the serpent said unto the woman, Ye shall not surely die. For God doth know that in the day ye eat thereof, then your eyes shall be opened, and ye shall be as gods, knowing good and evil, Gn 3:4 -5.***

And the reason this is important to understand is that Satan wants to ***be like God,*** as recorded in Isaiah fourteen. Satan uses people to try and accomplish his goal. Therefore, he knew if they obtained knowledge, they would be able to perform many marvelous wonders. Thereby, he convinces those he possesses to gain wisdom to mimic many of God's successes and achievements. Yet, when you pursue the same exploits, your goal is to impersonate the Lord-God of heaven; Scripture refers to this as sorcery! And the story of Moses verifies this!

How the story of Moses in Exodus twelve unfolded was when the Lord sent Moses to Pharaoh to release the children of Israel. At that time, the Lord God performed miracles through Aaron's rod. Pharaoh felt his kingdoms' achievements were of their makings and didn't believe in God. He couldn't comprehend how God was capable of creating miracles from a rod in Aaron's hand. Thereby,

Pharaoh went to the magicians and sorcerers and convinced them to copy the same marvels. Only when they couldn't produce the same miracle did Pharaoh allow Israel's children to leave, which he immediately regretted.

Then by understanding what sorcery means you should realize after they ate of the fruit from the tree of knowledge, the Lord said in Genesis three, verse twenty-two, and Genesis eleven, six, ***"Behold, the man has become as one of us, to know good and evil. Gn 3:22"*** The Lord was not naive and knew humankind would be capable of copying his achievements. Even after completing the tower of Babylon, ***the Lord said, Behold, the people is one, and they have all one language; and this they begin to do: and now nothing will be restrained from them, which they have imagined to do Gn 11:6***.

Eating from the tree of knowledge is the reason today, humankind has increased in wisdom and can mimic some of God's same achievements and even miracles. And by understanding this, it should be obvious the forbidden tree of knowledge changed humankind's makeup. This change enabled humanity's mind to evolve to the point we see on this day, and they can create medicine, which is for good and weapons of mass destruction for bad.

Nevertheless, when Christ came, he didn't bring medical books but healed people by God's power.

Even when ***Elijah called fire down from heaven***, it wasn't fireworks or planes dropping bombs, but God's power. Second Kings, chapter one, verse ten, tells the story.

And the New Testament testifies the Lord seeks those who have faith and trust in his power. In fact, ***without faith, it is impossible to please God, because anyone who comes to him must believe that he exists and that he rewards those who earnestly seek him, Hebrews 11:6.*** King James Bible.

Of course, during the days of the Roman Empire when the New Testament was written, they were not as advanced as they are today. However, the Jews and occupants of the Empire still accomplished many wonders during those days and couldn't fathom how evil spirits could inhabit them. After all, as mentioned before, they had gained wealth, fed the hungry, helped the poor, plus the Jews followed all the ordinances given to Mosses. As the years progressed, they began to put their trust in what was ***so-called science*** and testified in First Timothy six. Eventually, when a person was overcome and possessed by seven spirits, it was thought to be superstitious to believe in spirit possession, and mental illness took its place. At which point, the world became blind and unaware of this evil spirit's existence.

In fact, during Christ's day, an evil spirit in a man questioned Jesus ***if he had come to torment THEM before their time.***_Torment? Revealing Satan doesn't want to be cast into hell. Thereby, he deceives humankind in hopes of defeating the Lord-God. And apparently, this is the reason he assumed he needed the munitions that we see in this day, even creating a space force.

Christ's Second Coming

For you see, Scripture reveals when Christ comes again; He ***will come with the clouds of heaven.*** All reported in Mark fourteen: sixty-two. By gaining knowledge, Satan inhabits the earth's kings and their armies, and war will instill, and they will fight Christ at his second coming. However, this is Armageddon and the devil's last stand. ***And I saw the beast, and the kings of the earth, and their armies, gathered together to make war against him that sat on the horse, and against his army. And the beast was taken, and with him the false prophet that wrought miracles before him, with which he deceived them that had received the mark of the beast, and them that worshipped his image. These both were cast alive into a lake of fire burning with brimstone, Rv 19: 19,20.***

The world deceived, so when Revelation thirteen and Revelation seventeen explained, ***a beast would rise and it would have seven heads but these heads are actually mountains Rv 17:9.*** As we know, on this day, seven continents make up this world. And if you could visualize a continent rising out of the sea, you would know it is a vast mountain. And as revealed, it was this evil spirits' goal to deceive the entire world! But who could see?

Two Beasts and White horse

Then how all of this evolved from the time of Christ is written in Revelation thirteen and Revelation seventeen: nine, whereby this evil spirit used two leading players.

he first player or, as Revelation explains, the ***"first beast"*** was the Roman Empire. They were a people who didn't accept Christ's teachings, followed their philosophies, evil spirits possessing them, and were in Satan's throes. They persecuted the true Christians, and only God knows all the atrocities they put them through.

Satan, who is the God of this world, had blinded the minds of those who didn't believe. And how the story continued was John ***"saw one of his heads as it were wounded to death; and his deadly wound was healed: and all the world wondered after the beast Rv 13:3"***

You have to remember ***the beast has seven heads which are mountains Rv 17:9.*** And if you could visualize a continent rising out of the sea, you would know it is a vast mountain. A deceased mountain then basically explains how one of the continents populated by people who had been possessed by Satan would appear no more (dead). History then reveals how the Roman Empire faded away and seemed non-existent as she was no more.

After this, a second beast would rise.

Hence the second player is another beast or that being another deceiving evil spirit. The people he controls would assist in the first beasts' revival. To find this evil spirit we are then told to ***count the number of the beast: for it is the number of a man; and his number Six hundred threescore and six, Rv 13:18.*** How a number can be related to a man is how a person counts numbers and not in God's time. For example, if a man was born on January 6, 66, his name came into existence. Dates are universal, and God would want a person, regardless of where they lived in this world, to understand this number. Hence 666 years after Christ or the year was 666, the second beast or that deceiving spirit began its rise. During those days, the Catholic's changed the calendar twice to hide the year and made it difficult to pinpoint the exact date.

Revelation thirteen, eleven also explains the second beast would appear ***to be coming out of the earth, and he would have two horns like a lamb, and speak as a dragon.*** Having two horns of a lamb signifies two powers, and a lamb symbolizes Jesus. History reveals after the Roman Empire demise, there were two entities, the Catholics and the Protestants, which say they worship Jesus. At first, there was a lot of fighting between these two groups but bye and bye; they decided they all believed in the same God.

Nonetheless, Revelation explains this cunning spirit via the population he inhabits when coming forth would appear like one riding ***a white horse: and he that sat on him had a bow; and a crown was given unto him: and he went forth conquering, and to conquer Rv 6:2***. Revealing this spirit through humanity would appear as a beacon and do some good deeds as an angel of light. A white horse suggests purity and goodness, but it is a deceptive spirit riding forth in actuality. And when it came, it was to conquer. And this too was the reason we are warned that it was ***no marvel; for Satan himself is transformed into an angel of light, 2 Cor 11:14.***

History then reveals when the Catholic's and protestants came forth, they took lands, killing those who wouldn't believe in their God—even plundering the grounds of their gold and other resources. And not following Christ's teaching but used his name to deceive all. Even fighting amongst themselves for years.

Whereas, if they had followed what Christ taught, they would uphold his teachings. He told his apostles to, ***Go your ways: behold, I send you forth as lambs among wolves. Carry neither purse, nor scrip, nor shoes: and salute no man by the way. And into whatsoever house ye enter, first say, Peace be to this house. And if the son of peace be there, your peace shall rest upon it: if not, it shall turn to you again. And in the same house remain, eating and drinking such things as they give: for the labourer is worthy of his hire. Go not from house to house. And into whatsoever city ye enter, and they receive you, eat such things as are set before you: And heal the sick that are therein, and say unto them, The kingdom of God is come nigh unto you. But into whatsoever city ye enter, and they receive you not, go your ways out into the streets of the same, and say, Even the very dust of your city, which cleaveth on us, we do wipe off against you:***

notwithstanding be ye sure of this, that the kingdom of God is come nigh unto you. But I say unto you, that it shall be more tolerable in that day for Sodom, than for that city, Lk 10: 3-12.

Christ didn't send his apostles with guns blazing like these importers went forth. So, don't you see, in them, we can find ***the blood of prophets, and of saints, and of all that were slain upon the earth Rv 18:24.*** In fact, they manipulated the people, and committed genocide against the faithful saints. They even dispersed Israel, who was not even a nation again for two thousand years.

Sure, they claim they are like Daniel in Scripture, who was a man of war. During Daniel's days, the Jews were God's chosen people, and they were fighting for real estate, but we are living in the last days. And a day to God is like a thousand years. When Christ came, he explained God so ***loved the world*** and told us to do good unto our enemies that we are not to judge as he will. And He doesn't need our help! Look at the fires, tsunamis, volcanoes, plagues, and such.

On top of all that, John in Revelation explains when the second beast rose ***he exerciseth all the power of the first beast before him, and causeth the earth and them which dwell therein to worship the first beast, whose deadly wound was healed Rv 13:12.*** The Roman Empire was fierce, and by the power of its munitions, they ruled over many. Thus, so would this second deceiving evil spirit do.

Remember, the first beast was an evil spirit that inhabited the people that populated a nation. The second beast is another evil spirit that causes people to take this evil spirit into them, telling them this spirit is God. Don't you see how they provoked people to worship the beast (an evil spirit)?

Even the apostle warned the true church saying: ***Beloved, believe not every spirit, but try the spirits whether they are of God: because many false prophets are gone out into the world" 1 Jn 4:1.*** And to enable you to test a spirit, you have to know God is truth and ***the devil is a liar and the Father of it***, as testified in John eight, verse forty-four. For this reason, you can't take verses you like from Scripture and ignore the rest of the Bible. As Jesus explained in Matthew four, verse four, ***a man shall not live by bread alone but by Every Word of God***. And nobody could live by every Word of God if God was a hypocrite and didn't mean what He said throughout his Word. Therefore, if verses seem to contradict, pray until you understand.

Because second Corinthians eleven explains, apostate faiths would preach another Jesus, causing people to receive another spirit. And the reason Paul wrote, ***if he that cometh preacheth another Jesus, whom we have not preached, or if ye receive another spirit, which ye have not received, or another gospel, which ye have not accepted, ye might well bear with him. 2 Co 11:4.*** Hence, they ask another spirit in them and worship this spirit as God when it is the beast in actuality. ***And all that dwell upon the earth shall worship him, whose names are not written in the book of life of the Lamb slain from the foundation of the world. If any man has an ear, let him hear Rv 13:8.***

Red Horse

So, by and by, this spirit by way of man eventually progressed to the point he could invent planes, bombs and accomplished many great wonders. ***And he doeth great wonders, so that he maketh fire come down from heaven on the earth in the sight of men, Rv 13:3.***

WWI and WWII reveal the next prophesy in Revelation six when they finalized their conquest.

Whereby we're told of another horse that was red in color: ***and power was given to him that sat thereon to take peace from the earth, and that they should kill one another: and there was given unto him a great sword.*** Making weapons of mass destruction and even selling them to the highest bidder. Promoting war, strife, and killing.

Red was the color of those days; Hitler was even flying his red flags. And the wars caused red blood to flow from one continent to the other.

But no one was as great as the second beast. With the finest military and mighty munitions which caused people to say, ***"Who is like*** this movement***? Who is able to make war with him? Rv 13:4"***

And once they had accomplished all these feats, they were like a chameleon; they portrayed themselves as the persecuted and God's saints. Thereby changing the truth of Scripture into philosophies and ***interpretations being***

their laws and seasons. All prophesied in Daniel, chapter seven, verse twenty-five.

So, I hope you see, the first beast was a city being the Roman Empire whose occupants were inhabited by an evil spirit. She influenced the entire known world at that time. The second beast will make an image that would be a likeness of the first beast. Thereby, the image created would be a city (nation) of people inhabited by an evil spirit who would influence the entire world. It would rule with an iron hand being their munitions, and all who would not bow to her were sanctioned and killed. So, don't you see as Revelation proclaims, ***the woman which thou sawest is that great city, which reigneth over the kings of the earth Rv 17:3***—also called Babylon in another chapter.

Whom do you believe?

You have a choice, you can believe Scripture when it explains, ***we wrestle not against flesh and blood, but against principalities, against powers, against the rulers of the darkness of this world, against spiritual wickedness in high places,*** and written in Ephesians six.

One of the only signs we will get in these last days is those who become crazy and do unspeakable acts like shootings, bombings, etc. All because they didn't believe in Jesus. As this is when ***the unclean spirit is gone out of a man, he walks through dry places, seeking rest, and finds none. Then he saith, I will return into my house from whence I came out; and when he is come, he finds***

it empty, swept, and garnished. Then he takes with him seven other spirits more wicked than himself, and they enter in this man and dwell there: and the last state of that man is worse than the first. Even so shall it be also unto this wicked generation Rv 12:43-45.

Thereby, do you want to put your trust in a man who assumes we evolved from monkeys? Where is their proof?

We can prove a boy turns into a man as we can witness and watch it happen. But a monkey changing into a man?

A monkey progressing to the point he can fly a space ship to the moon? Or an astronomical string of events and coincidentally, everything from humankind to every animal was just accidentally created?

Yet what I know is mankind in their infancy, stole the fruit from a tree that enabled them to learn, both good and evil. This fruit allowed humans to mature to heal the sick and is good and make bombs that can kill for the bad.

If humanity can fly a spaceship to the moon, why wouldn't the Lord God, who created the entire world, have a tree with fruit that would enable mankind to evolve?

Eons ago, before Noah and the flood. Why couldn't there have been a serpent that talked? Or was it because an evil spirit inhabited the snake, enabling it to talk? Either way, ***God is true and all men are liars*** as testified in Romans three verse four. I thereby have written this little book with the scriptures.

CHAPTER 3

THE MEANING OF DEATH

THE FALLING AWAY

Two thousand years ago, Christ called the so-called religions ***a den of thieves.*** And the reason he said that was because they steal what they want from Scripture, and make merchandise out of those who follow them. These frauds reassure heaven to those who give them money like this will save their soul.

And before we look at the rest of Revelation, it will be essential to see how apostate faiths have turned everything upside down. To the point, people don't understand who Christ is, who God is, and what death is.

So, to begin with, and written in Geneses one, the Lord said to those in heaven, ***"Let us make man in OUR image, after our likeness Gn 1:26."*** The Lord God was speaking to the angels in heaven, and many scriptures reveal we look like those in heaven.

One instance that reveals, in appearance, we look like the angels or that being people who live in heaven was when ***there came two angels to Sodom at even; and Lot sat in the gate of Sodom: and Lot seeing them rose up to meet them; and he bowed himself with his face toward the ground; And he said, Behold now, my lords, turn in, I pray you, into your servant's house, and tarry all night, and wash your feet, and ye shall rise up early, and go on your ways. And they said, Nay; but we will abide in the street all night. And he pressed upon them greatly; and they turned in unto him, and entered into his house; and he made them a feast, and did bake unleavened bread, and they did eat. Gn 19: 1-3***

But before they lay down, the men of the city, even the men of Sodom, compassed the house round, both old and young, all the people from every quarter: And they called unto Lot, and said unto him, Where are the men which came in to thee this night? bring them out unto us, that we may know them. Gn 19: 4,5

So, you see, the townspeople assumed these angels were men who came into town and didn't realize they were on a mission from heaven. Whereby revealing angels, which are people from heaven in appearance, look like men.

Another example of how people on earth resemble those from heaven was when Daniel spoke to an angel from heaven. Daniel ten, verse eighteen, explains he was sitting by a brook when he tells us that *there came a person who appeared as a man*, but this was an angel.

We are forewarned not to, ***Be not forgetful to entertain strangers: for thereby some have entertained angels unawares, Hb 13:2.*** Again, we could meet a stranger, and the stranger might have been an angel. Proving again, those from heaven look like those of us upon the earth.

Even first Corinthians fifteen, verse thirty-five through forty-nine; reveals: "***There are also celestial bodies, and bodies terrestrial: but the glory of the celestial is one, and the glory of the terrestrial is another 1 Co 15:40".***

The difference between terrestrial and celestial; is that people on earth look like those in heaven, yet the type of flesh is different in character and composition.

Understanding how the Bible teaches people on earth look like those in heaven. After Christ rose from the dead, we find they went to his gravesite, and it was empty. As recorded, ***they entered in, and found not the body of the Lord Jesus. And it came to pass, as they were much perplexed thereabout, behold, two men stood by them in shining garments: Lk 24: 3,4.***

His grave empty was also noted when two angels were standing by his gravesite, dressed in shiny clothes. Showing us again, Angels look like people. Although in this case they were dressed a bit conspicuously.

Some days later, the apostles were discussing the events that had taken place when ***Jesus himself stood in the midst of them, and saith unto them, Peace be unto you. But they were terrified and affrighted, and supposed that***

they had seen a spirit. And he said unto them, Why are ye troubled? and why do thoughts arise in your hearts? Behold my hands and my feet, that it is I myself: handle me, and see; for a spirit hath not flesh and bones, as ye see me have. And when he had thus spoken, he shewed them his hands and his feet. Lk 24:36-40. Christ himself denied he was a ghost or a spirit. So, you see, a celestial body, is what Christ rose in from the grave.

In other words, the Spirit of God in Christ changed Jesus. As Jesus explained before his crucifixion, ***Verily, verily, I say unto thee, Except a man be born again, he cannot see the kingdom of God Jn 3:3. That which is born of the flesh is flesh; and that which is born of the Spirit is spirit. Marvel not that I said unto thee, Ye must be born again. Jn 3:6-7.***

Even Paul told us ***if the Spirit of him that raised up Jesus from the dead dwell in you, he that raised up Christ from the dead shall also <u>quicken your mortal bodies</u> by his Spirit that dwelleth in you, Rom 8:11.*** Revealing Christ crucified, while in the grave, the Spirit of God in him accomplished the rebirth. And he was clothed with a celestial body.

Christ rose, was restored, and reborn into a heavenly body. His death was similar to a caterpillar that goes into a cocoon and changes into a butterfly. Once changed, he rose from the grave, and his tomb was empty. To be born again is to be made into *a new creature* by God's Spirit whereby the tabernacle, being our body, will be changed. All testified in Second Corinthians five.

First, Corinthians testifies our ***body is the temple of the Holy Ghost, 1 Co 6:19.*** Thereby like Christ, we are two people in one body. Us being the first person and the Holy Spirit being the second person. And without a body, we would not have a temple and be separated from our God (His Holy Spirit).

For this corruptible must put on incorruption, and this mortal must put on immortality. So when this corruptible shall have put on incorruption, and this mortal shall have put on immortality, then shall be brought to pass the saying that is written, Death is swallowed up in victory. O death, where is thy sting? O grave, where is thy victory? 1 Co 15:53-55

Christ's Second coming

And we know when Christ comes back it will be in judgment. ***And then shall appear the sign of the Son of man in heaven: and then shall all the tribes of the earth mourn, and they shall see the Son of man coming in the clouds of heaven with power and great glory. Mt 24:30***

Even those who remain faithful will be transformed at Christ's appearing ***in the twinkling of an eye 1 Co 15:52.*** For you see, our body is the temple (house), and the Holy Spirit resides in us. Revealing the Holy Spirit within us will change our body too.

As mentioned before: ***if the Spirit of him that raised up Jesus from the dead dwell in you, he that raised up***

Christ from the dead shall also quicken your mortal bodies by his Spirit that dwelleth in you, Rom 8:11. In other words, the Spirit of God in us will stimulate our dying bodies to live, and we'll be born again by the Spirit.

Thereby, the true meaning of death is to suffer separation from God. Because once you lose your body, your soul will not die as Christ referred to the soul as a worm. In a sense, it cannot go to sleep but obviously cannot find rest. ***Such people will suffer the punishment of eternal destruction by being separated from the Lord's presence and from his glorious power, 1 Thes 1:9*** International Standard Bible

Test the Spirits to See if he proceeds from God

As Christ proclaimed, ***God is a spirit Jn 4:24.*** Thereby, God and Satan are spirits, so it is important not to believe ***every spirit, but try the spirits whether they are of God: because many false prophets are gone out into the world 1 Jn 4:1.***

Many people claim Jesus is God; however, I want to be emphatic that you understand we don't follow ***Satan who wants to be like God.*** Christ told us ***God is a Spirit***. And after Christ rose from the dead, he said to the apostles, ***Behold my hands and my feet, that it is I myself: handle me, and see; for a spirit hath not flesh and bones, as ye see me have, Lk 24:39.***

Since the beginning of time, the Serpent was able to deceive Adam and Eve, claiming they wouldn't die even if they lost their body, and they turned into dust.

Albeit Christ explained in Mark nine, verse forty-eight saying that it is true that our soul will not die even if we lose our body. He mentioned our soul could be cast into hell where we would suffer torment.

Christ's tomb was empty, but Adam and Eve, unlike Christ, ***returned unto the ground; for out of it they were taken: for dust they were, and unto dust they returned Gn 3:19.***

Even Paul asked, ***"What? know ye not that your body is the temple of the Holy Ghost which is in you? 1 Co 6:15"*** If you had realized our body is the temple of God's Holy Spirit, wouldn't you recognize without a body there is no temple? Whereby, if the temple of God's Holy Spirit is our body and it turns into dust like Adam and Eve, then we would be separated from God's Holy Spirit and dead! Thereby, like unto Satan, who is unable to find rest, would our soul also wander?

Paul speaking of Christ's second coming, said, ***"Beloved, now are we the sons of God, and it doth not yet appear what we shall be: but we know that, when he shall appear, we shall be like him; for we shall see him as he is 1 Jn 3:2."*** So again, we will be like Christ and not God, who is a Spirit.

If we have received God's Spirit, our body by the Spirit of God will accomplish the final stages of the rebirth, and we too would be clothed with a celestial body. And will be saved from death.

As I dare to repeat, as Paul reassured us saying: ***if the Spirit of him that raised up Jesus from the dead dwell in you, he that raised up Christ from the dead shall also quicken your mortal bodies by his Spirit that dwelleth in you, Rom 8:11.*** In other words, the Spirit of God in us will stimulate our dying bodies to live, and we'll be born again by the Spirit. It doesn't mention a different body but the mortal body we inhabit is changed.

Losing your body, you have you lost the house the Holy Spirit lives in. Not to mention your soul is released and left to wander.

We don't follow Adam but Christ, whose tomb was empty.

And proving this is true, we will look at another story in the New Testament. During the days of the Roman Empire, they were on a quest to commit genocide against the true church. At that time, they had killed James, the brother of John, and had captured Peter.

Peter therefore was kept in prison: but prayer was made without ceasing of the church unto God for him. And when Herod would have brought him forth, the same night Peter was sleeping between two soldiers, bound with two chains: and the keepers before the door kept the prison Acts 12: 5,6.

And, behold, the angel of the Lord came upon him, and a light shined in the prison: and he smote Peter on the side, and raised him up, saying, Arise up quickly. And his chains fell off from his hands, Act 12: 7

And the angel said unto him, Gird thyself, and bind on thy sandals. And so he did. And he saith unto him, Cast thy garment about thee, and follow me. And he went out, and followed him; and wist not that it was true which was done by the angel; but thought he saw a vision, Acts 12: 8-9.

When they were past the first and the second ward, they came unto the iron gate that leadeth unto the city; which opened to them of his own accord: and they went out, and passed on through one street; and forthwith the angel departed from him. And when Peter was come to himself, he said, Now I know of a surety, that the Lord hath sent his angel, and hath delivered me out of the hand of Herod, and from all the expectation of the people of the Jews Acts 12: 10-11

Before they realized what had happened, they assumed Peter had been killed and resurrected. Thereby, they thought Peter had been transformed and was coming to them from heaven.

For you see, we don't believe in death and know if we follow Christ, we will follow him in his resurrection as promised. For Christ testified and said, ***he that believeth in me, though he were dead, yet shall he live Jn 11:25.*** And as we all know, Christ's grave was empty; and the apostles even ate with him after he rose from the grave. All testified in Mark sixteen, chapter fourteen. Therefore, this is the promise unto those who believe him.

THE FALSE PROPHET IS A HYPOCRITE

Christ was speaking to the religious leaders in that day when he said: ***"The thief comes not, but for to steal, and to kill, and to destroy: I am come that they might have life, and that they might have it more abundantly, Jn 10:10."*** Calling them thieves was because they steal people's money, promising those who follow them heaven—appearing like angels of light, they cause people to be unaware. While on the other hand, the Lord gives those in Christ what they need and life eternal, which is more than abundant.

I would say the same is true for those in these days. And this is not because I judge, but because I believe Christ. However, those who are greedy read abundant life, claim Christ meant riches and wealth. ***For such are false apostles, deceitful workers, transforming themselves into the apostles of Christ, 2 Cor 11:13.*** For these are those Christ warned of and said to, ***"Take heed, and beware of covetousness: for a man's life consists not in the abundance of the things which he possesses Lk 12:15."***

CHAPTER 4

Knowing God and Jesus

To know God is true is the only way you are going to find eternal life. At which point, you will also realize God sent Jesus Christ, and he is the one who exposed the truth. This is not what I think but what Christ told us in John seventeen, verse three, yet no one gets it.

Everyone knows about Christ and God, but they sure don't know Christ told the truth. Thereby, those that came preached another Jesus, teaching you can live like the devil and still go to heaven, 2 Cor 11:3. Which is a lie from hell. In fact, Christ said: ***He that rejecteth me*** (hears not what Christ said)***, and receiveth*** (follows) ***not my words*** (teachings)***, hath one that judgeth him: the word that I have spoken, the same shall judge him in the last day Jn 12:48.***

So, to understand who Jesus and who God is, we will have to look into another dimension.

When I was traveling around the world, I found no one could explain who God is. Sure, some would draw a triangle calling one side father, one side son, and the other side god. Others would say God is a force, power, etc. Even others claim he is some guy in heaven.

Everyone knows about Christ, but who knows who Christ is? And again, it is for this reason; it will be essential to understand how, First Corinthians starting at chapter fifteen in verse twelve, explains how a human body can be either ***celestial or terrestrial***. A terrestrial person is of the earth while a heavenly person would be of heaven; they look similar, yet somehow, each is different.

To understand how we look like those in heaven, we can find another book in Scripture that verifies this. It was when Jacob was alienated from his brother Esau. The story about Jacob estranged from his brother is located in the Old Testament, and as boys, Jacob had hijacked Esau's birthright. Jacob knew Esau was angry with him, so he fled his native land and lived and worked for a man called Laban. Laban was a harsh taskmaster, but the Lord blessed Jacob. Laban meant to use Jacob like a slave, yet Jacob prospered, and he gained most of Laban's wealth. The Lord helped Jacob by acquiring most of Laban's livestock, which angered Laban's sons, who wanted vengeance. Yet, because the Lord was with Jacob, He told him to return home from where he fled.

Returning home, Jacob was concerned Esau would hold a grudge against him and even want to kill him. Nonetheless, as the Lord commanded, he traveled back to his hometown when God's angels met him.

At first, it doesn't appear Jacob was aware the men he met were angels. Later that night, it's not written why Jacob wrestled with one of these men, but he wrestled with one.

And, apparently, in those days, men would bestow a blessing on others they challenged. And Jacob realized the type of divine sanction he received could only be given to him by God's angel and not a man. So again, we find those in heaven appear like men and not wind—written in Geneses thirty-two.

Like unto the angels in heaven, Christ is also a celestial being, as the previous chapter from Scripture revealed. God on the other hand, ***is a Spirit: and they that worship him must worship him in spirit and in truth, Jn 4:24.*** To worship in spirit is to glorify God with your entire being and not because you are a ghost. You couldn't worship God on earth if that were the case.

Then how Christ's story unfolds is to realize God who's physical being is a spirit, and the Word is what He says, due to He created the world by what He said—speaking everything into existence.

Thereby the God-head which is where all of God's power comes from. Thus, when this power is released it is via words and what He says comes into being. Thereby when God said, "***Let there be a firmament in the midst of the waters, and let it divide the waters from the waters, Gn***

1:6. What God pronounces comes into being He doesn't transform himself into what He communicated.

The way the Bible explains this spiritual dimension is by telling us; ***For as the body is one, and hath many members, and all the members of that one body, being many, are one body: so also is Christ, 1Cor 12:12.***

For by one Spirit are we all baptized into one body, whether we be Jews or Gentiles, whether we be bond or free; and have been all made to drink into one Spirit, 1Cor 12:13.

For the body is not one member, but many, 1Cor 12:14.

In other words, our body is like a house the Holy Spirit dwells in. Now the Holy Spirit is one Spirit and although He is in many people it is somehow connected. Scripture explained God's Spirit, like that of a body, which consists of many body parts. Hands, feet, legs, arms, etc.

So, what I am going to do is include an illustration of how the Spirit of God works in us. In other words, we (body and soul) are the temple (house)

Realizing we are the house God's Spirit dwells in if you had spiritual eyes, this illustration is what the Kingdom of God would look like in its entirety. Due to those in Christ receive of God's Spirit, which is one Spirit.

Of course, we see a person in reality, and only a portion of God's Spirit is in him or her.

Then like our brain controls our body, the God-Head is the portion of God's Spirit that is in charge of the rest of His Spirit. This portion of God's Spirit is the Father and He is in Christ and this is what will be explained next.

Jesus is the Messiah and the portion of God's Spirit in him would be the highest-ranking allocation.

Now the way the story of Christ unfolds is to understand: ***In the beginning was the Word, and the Word was with God, and the Word was God. The same*** (Jesus) ***was in the beginning with God. All things were made by him; and without him was not any thing made that was made. In him was life; and the life was the light of men.***

And the light shineth in darkness; and the darkness comprehended it not, Jn 1:1-5.

The world created, Christ was a celestial being in heaven, and the allocated portion of God's Holy Spirit that dwelled in Christ was the superior portion of God's Holy Spirit. The Godhead portion is like the root of a tree and supplies strength and power to the tree. Thereby, when the Lord created the earth, Christ was directed by the Holy Ghost within him to say***, Let there be light,*** and it was so. So God in Christ spoke and the words God pronounced through Christ came into being. Not, God, a Spirit changes into what He communicates, but what he articulates comes into existence.

Then Christ's birth came about in like fashion, whereas the Word of God, which is God's Spirit, spoke and said, let my beloved Son be born flesh. Hence, the angel of God came unto Mary and explained how the ***Holy Ghost,*** which is Christ's Father, ***would come upon her and she would be with child, Lk 1:35.*** Thereby, God's word spoken Mary was found with child.

At which point Jesus in heaven with a celestial body, changed form, and became an embryo and was implanted in Mary. The portion of God's Holy Spirit in Christ was the sovereign portion of God's Spirit being the Father, and He stayed in heaven.

Thereby, Christ was born a terrestrial man and ***was in all points tempted like as we are, yet without sin, Heb 4:15.*** On the other hand***, God cannot be tempted by evil*** as

Jesus was; thereby, God could not become flesh! All testified in James one verse thirteen.

At the time of the birth of Jesus, Israel was ruled by king Herod the Great. He was known for his great building projects and his and ruthlessness. During that day, they rebuilt Jerusalem along with the temple. Even though it was a perplexing time.

The religious understood the book of Daniel told them the rebuilding of the city and temple would take sixty years, and the Messiah would come. At which point, many were going out and being baptized by John the Baptist.

The prophecy in Daniel read; Know ***therefore and understand, that from the going forth of the commandment to restore and to build Jerusalem unto the Messiah the Prince shall be seven weeks, and threescore and two weeks: the street shall be built again, and the wall, even in troublous times, Dn 9:25.***

The Jews that believed the Book of Daniel; expected Christ to appear and were baptized by John the Baptist. ***As it is written in the prophets, Behold, I send my messenger before thy face, which shall prepare thy way before thee, Mk 1:2.***

Also, as prophecy predicted, John was, ***The voice of one crying in the wilderness, Prepare ye the way of the Lord, make his paths straight. John did baptize in the wilderness, and preach the baptism of repentance for the remission of sins. And there went out unto him all***

the land of Judaea, and they of Jerusalem, and were all baptized of him in the river of Jordan, confessing their sins, Mk 1: 3-4.

Then the gospel of Mark illustrates how Jesus came about receiving the Holy Spirit. The way the story unfolds in Scripture was prior to Jesus beginning his ministry. Whereby, ***it came to pass in those days, that Jesus came from Nazareth of Galilee, and was baptized of John in Jordan. And straightway coming up out of the water, he saw the heavens opened, and the Spirit like a dove descending upon him: And there came a voice from heaven, saying, Thou art my beloved Son, in whom I am well pleased. And immediately the spirit driveth him into the wilderness, Mark 1:9-12.***

Next you have to, of course, believe Christ when he told us that God is a Spirit. And that a Spirit is capable of speaking. Thereby, from heaven, the Father declared Jesus was His Son. The Holy Spirit Christ received at that time is attached to the Father yet a separate entity.

The Spirit of God and how the Spirit is assembled can be challenging to understand. Another analogy is to take a tree for an example. The origin of a tree's power is its root, and it supplies all its power to the tree. The Father is like the tree's root, while the rest of his body (Holy Spirit) is like the tree.

Once Christ had finished telling us what the Father gave him to reveal, most of the population hated him and crucified him. While Christ was in the grave for three days, his body went through a life cycle known as complete metamorphosis. Similar to what a butterfly would experience. Consequently, his earthly body changed back into the heavenly. He put on immortality, and the rebirth (born again) took witness. Thereby, resurrected, and his ***grave was empty.*** All testified in First Corinthians fifteen: fifty-one thru fifty-four.

Now because Christ lives, He revealed before his crucifixion that He is the Messiah. Before they executed him on the cross, Christ prayed to the Father saying: ***"And now, O Father, glorify thou me with thine own self with the glory which I had with thee before the world was, Jn 17:5."*** Revealing, he would receive the highest-ranking portion of God's Holy Spirit. As this portion of God's Spirit was in him before his birth. God then glorified Jesus with himself, which is our Father. For Christ loved, ***righteousness, and hated wickedness. Therefore God, your God, has anointed you with the oil of gladness above your fellows, Psm 45:7.***

And this is the reason Jesus told us ***he that hath seen me hath seen the Father, Jn 14:9.*** And this again, was because once Jesus rose back into heaven, the Father anointed him with himself. Of course, you can't see a ghost but have the realization they are two people in one body.

Receiving the Father in him was the reason Christ said, ***at that day ye shall know that I am in my Father, and ye in me, and I in you Jn 14:20.*** Meaning the Supreme portion of God's Spirit entered him, and the Holy Spirit we received was a part of the Holy Spirit that was in Christ when He walked upon the earth.

Or in other words, Christ is the temple of God's Holy Spirit, and the highest-ranking portion of God's Spirit entered back into him once resurrected.

Thereby after Christ had risen, he received the Father back into him, and the portion of the Holy Spirit that had been in Jesus when He walked upon earth is now dispersed and goes into the saints of God. Whereby he is in us.

Hence the Father in him and he is in us. Our goal is not to be like God who is a Spirit but like Jesus, as written in first John chapter three. ***Beloved, now are we the sons of God, and it doth not yet appear what we shall be: but we know that, when he shall appear, we shall be like him; for we shall see him as he is, Jn 1:2.***

Christ, a celestial being is our Lord, and the Spirit in him is our God.

So, you see, our body is the temple where God's Spirit dwells. Neither shall they say, ***Lo here! or, lo there! for, behold, the kingdom of God is within you, Lk 17:21***. Possessed by God's Spirit, we are two people in one body, which is the lamb's marriage.

The Abomination of Desolation

After Christ was assassinated, Daniel explains: ***after threescore and two weeks shall Messiah be cut off, but not for himself: and the people of the prince that shall come shall destroy the city and the sanctuary; and the***

end thereof shall be with a flood, and unto the end of the war desolations are determined, Dn 9:26.

Cut off means he would be crucified, yet because he lives, he would not be cut off to those who believe him. And this is not to mean they only believe he existed but what he taught!

Thereby Jerusalem did not exist for two thousand years, the temple destroyed, and the apostasy rose. Even Christ explained this, when he told the apostles after they, ***departed from the temple: and his disciples came to him for to shew him the buildings of the temple. And Jesus said unto them, See ye not all these things? verily I say unto you, There shall not be left here one stone upon another, that shall not be thrown down, Mt 24:1, 2.*** Of course, Christ was speaking of that temple not some new temple they have fabricated in this day.

Additionally, ***as he sat upon the mount of Olives, the disciples came unto him privately, saying, Tell us, when shall these things be? and what shall be the sign of thy coming, and of the end of the world? And Jesus answered and said unto them, Take heed that no man deceive you, Mt 24:3, 4.*** Then Christ went on to tell them to be careful and not be deceived. ***For many shall come in my name, saying, I am Christ; and shall deceive many, Mt 24:5.*** They admit Jesus in the Christ but don't follow his teachings.

For there shall arise false Christs, and false prophets, and shall shew great signs and wonders; insomuch that, if

it were possible, they shall deceive the very elect. Behold, I have told you before. Wherefore if they shall say unto you, Behold, he is in the desert; go not forth: behold, he is in the secret chambers; believe it not. Mt 24: 24-26.

Then when we read Daniel we find out after, ***the daily sacrifice shall be taken away, and the abomination that maketh desolate set up, there shall be a thousand two hundred and ninety days, Dn 12:11.*** Of course the daily sacrifice was done away with when they tore down that temple. Whereby the sin that brought ruin upon the souls of people was those who claimed they could lead you to Christ. Causing people to take a spirit into them but it was actually another spirit (the beast). I suppose the thousand two hundred and ninety days in that verse are years but then Scripture tells us those days would be shortened and no one would really be able to pinpoint the exact time.

Nonetheless, ***When ye therefore shall see the abomination of desolation, spoken of by Daniel the prophet, stand in the holy place, (whoso readeth, let him understand:), Mt 24:15.*** If my understanding is correct, this evil spirit would stand in place of the holy. And when this evil spirit is made known and revealed there will be a great tribulation.

In fact, Daniel thirteen, verse eight in the New International Bible called it the rebellion that caused desolation. And Babylon the Great is called the abominations of the earth in Revelation seventeen, verse five.

Thereby, ***Then let them which be in Judaea flee into the mountains: Let him which is on the housetop not come down to take any thing out of his house: Neither let him which is in the field return back to take his clothes. And woe unto them that are with child, and to them that give suck in those days! But pray ye that your flight be not in the winter, neither on the sabbath day: For then shall be great tribulation, such as was not since the beginning of the world to this time, no, nor ever shall be, Mt 24:16:21.***

FOOTNOTE

On the other hand, those who receive God's Holy Spirit would realize we are no longer one person but two. Therefore, fornication is the only sin to the body. Otherwise, we would drag the Holy Spirit into the act with us. Scripture says it this way: ***Flee fornication. Every sin that a man doeth is without the body; but he that committeth fornication sinneth against his own body, 1 Cor 6:18.***

Many support pro-life and are against abortion. Fornication is the sin. Children born out of wedlock are the fruit of the sin. If they were pro-life, wouldn't they preach the truth?

TEST THE SPIRITS

There is a way which seemeth right unto a man, but the end thereof are the ways of death, Prv 14:12. Solomon was saying; you can give to the poor, help the needy, and do all kinds of good works. On the surface, all of this is good, but none of these works will buy you a ticket into heaven.

For by grace are ye saved through faith; and that not of yourselves: it is the gift of God: Not of works, lest any man should boast Eph 2: 8,9. Faith is to trust God's Word, believe in God's Word, and know that He is truth. To be a doer of the Word and not just a hearer is not the works mentioned in Ephesians. Neither does grace mean you can live like the devil and expect paradise.

James was a saint of God and lived when the Church was under great persecution. To endure, he had suffered many hardships. Writing via the Spirit of God, James explained a person has to be a doer of God's Word. Thereby when he said: ***Yea, a man may say, Thou hast faith, and I have works: shew me thy faith without thy works, and I will shew thee my faith by my works Jms 2:18.*** He meant through all of his hardships, he took no bribes, lived not in fornication, took no vengeance on those who showed revenge, and when persecuted, he was able to turn his cheek. He loved those who loved him not and fought the good fight. This was the faith Christ taught.

For there was nothing written in Scripture that was in vain, and the New Testament testifies the Lord seeks those who have faith and trust in his Word, which is his Power. ***But without faith it is impossible to please him: for he that cometh to God must believe that he is, and that he is a rewarder of them that diligently seek him Heb 11:6.***

Don't you see, our God is Holy, and our God is a Spirit as Christ professed, thus unlike Satan, our God is a Holy Spirit. ***Our God is not a man, that he should lie and neither is he the Son of man, that he should repent Nu 23:19.*** So how could Jesus be God if he came as a man in the flesh? ***Hereby know ye the Spirit of God: Every spirit that confesseth that Jesus Christ is come in the flesh is of God, 1 Jn 4:2.***

In fact, ***All Scripture is given by inspiration of God, and is profitable for doctrine, for reproof, for correction, for instruction in righteousness, 2 Tim 3:16.*** When written, the Bible was directed by the Holy Spirit that resided in God's saints and not their private interpretation. Whereby when God's Spirit leads a person, they would not contradict others that wrote other books of the Bible because God is not a hypocrite.

On the other hand, a hypocrite will assume one chapter says one thing, and another chapter means something else. Contradicting Bible chapters is the reason Christ told us to get the log out of our eyes. ***Thou hypocrite, first cast out the beam out of thine own eye; and then shalt thou see clearly to cast out the mote out of thy brother's eye, Jn 7:5.***

Because when you believe Christ, you realize the Bible is the Word of God, and He is not a liar or wishy-washy.

And I hope you see; this is how we can test spirits to see if they are of God.

For we know if God's Spirit guides a person, they would adhere to every Word that comes from the Bible, as testified in Matthew four, verse four. On the other hand, a person directed by a deceptive spirit may use Scripture and tricks the unsuspecting by double meanings.

One tremendous example of how Satan's apostles turn God's Word into double meanings is when Eve was in Eden. When the Lord took the man, He put him in the garden to ***dress it and to keep it Gn 2:15. And the Lord God commanded the man, saying, Of every tree of the garden thou mayest freely eat: But of the tree of the knowledge of good and evil, thou shalt not eat of it: for in the day that thou eatest thereof thou shalt surely die, Gn 2:16, 17.***

However, when Satan comes along, he said, unto the woman, ***"Yea, hath God said, Ye shall not eat of every tree of the garden, Gn 3:1?*** The Lord said they could eat of every tree, but you will die when you eat from the forbidden tree. So, Satan basically said if you can eat of every tree like the Lord said, ***"Ye shall not surely die: For God doth know that in the day ye eat thereof, then your eyes shall be opened, and ye shall be as gods, knowing good and evil, Gn 3:2-5."***

Catching this evil spirit's mode of operation, we find Satan's apostles use God's words to deceive by explaining what a person likes to hear but refuses and denies everything else the Lord said.

Additionally, in the New Testament, Christ is always calling the religious leaders' hypocrites. As they, too, would use a verse in Scripture and ignore verses that seem to have the exception to the rule. God is not a hypocrite, and Christ always called the religious leaders out on this. All because they didn't consider every word in Scripture. Christ didn't judge them, but recognized they were hypocrites by the way they understood Scripture.

And because Christ always called them out for being hypocrites, they thought they would trick him and reveal he did the same thing. How this transpired, there was a day Christ via the Spirit of God in him, healed a sick man and how the story goes: Jesus ***entered again into the synagogue; and there was a man there which had a withered hand. And they watched him, whether he would heal him on the sabbath day; that they might accuse him. And he saith unto the man which had the withered hand, Stand forth. And he saith unto them, Is it lawful to do good on the sabbath days, or to do evil? to save life, or to kill? But they held their peace, Mk 3: 1-4.***

In that day the religious tried to incriminate Christ as they knew, the sabbath is for rest and not work. Thereby insinuating if God was not a hypocrite why did Jesus heal on the sabbath. Of course, God shines his sun on the sabbath, and He doesn't hold it back from anyone. So why wouldn't God's Spirit via Christ heal someone on the Sabbath day too?

Yet, by seeing all of these examples, I hope you understand how a person can use Scripture out of context. As another example in this day, we find people claim Jesus is

God. They even say they have three Gods, being the Father, Son, and Holy Ghost. But if you believe Scripture. How can this be true? How can Jesus be God? When Numbers explains, ***God is not the Son of man*, *Nu 23:19.*** And Christ is not only the Son of God but also called himself the Son of man in Scripture! Do you believe the word of God or what people say?

Then Scripture testifies ***no one has ever seen God at any time,1 Jn 1:18.*** Didn't people see Christ? How could he be God?

Much less, how could Satan tempt God? After all, Christ went out into the wilderness, and like Satan promised Adam and Eve life! The devil promised Christ a kingship over the world. We all would be in trouble if God would give up his glory for Satan!

God's words are in the Bible, but when a person doesn't believe them, he turns God into a liar. And how the Bible says this same thing is as follows: ***"He that believes not God hath made him a liar, 1 Jn 5:10".*** In other words, a person who doesn't believe the Word of God; will turn the Word of God being the Bible into lies by contradicting what it says.

I can't stress it enough. You must test the spirits a person may be following! But when you examine the teachings, you have to believe and know God is true, or how else could you live by every Word found in the Bible? For God is not like Satan, a liar, and He doesn't have double meanings to try and trick or confuse those who believe him.

ANTICHRIST

We know that we know Him, if we keep His commandments. He who says, "I know Him," and does not keep His commandments, is a liar, and the truth is not in him. But whoever keeps His word, truly the love of God perfected in him. By this we know that we are in Him. He who says he abides in Him ought himself also to walk just as He walked, 1 Jn 2: 3-6. Obviously, nobody is perfect, but we know if we continue to be disobedient, we cannot consider ourselves blessed when the letters to the churches in Revelation verifies this. Neither can we deliberately live in sin and assume we will find grace.

According to some movies they would sacrifice a virgin and throw him into a volcano thinking this would save them from the volcano gods. In this day I have found those with this same mind-set. They claim Jesus was nothing more than a virgin sacrificed on the cross. So now the blood he shed will save them from the God of heaven.

The reason God required a sacrifice was because he can't lie. In other words, what God says has to come to fruition. Hence death was pronounced upon all when Adam and Eve disobeyed God.

On the other hand, Christ was perfect and didn't disobey God. And because Christ was perfect, he didn't have to die. But he chose to take our sins upon him and die in our place.

Thereby, God didn't lie as we died with Christ. But the second part of that equation is we died with Christ as long as we followed him and his teachings.

Adam and Eve could eat from any tree in the Garden of Eden. The second part of that equation was if they ate from the Tree of Knowledge they would die.

And the reason Christ didn't have to die and go to hell like Adam and Eve even though death was pronounced upon all. Was because he was perfect and without sin. It's kind of like an algebra problem: obedience + obedience = Life. Or - disobedience + - disobedience = death. And because we aren't perfect, we rely on following Christ's teachings thereby he died in our place and was three days in the grave.

Then if you can comprehend that Jesus is two people in one body, you will understand the reason First John two, verse twenty-two, explains, ***"Who is a liar but he that denieth that Jesus is the Christ? He is antichrist, that denieth the Father and the Son, 1 Jn 2:22".*** In other words, Jesus is anointed by the sovereign portion of God's Holy Spirit, thereby making him the Christ.

For example, if John lives in a house, you don't call the building John lives in, John, do you? Or if a woman is carrying a baby they previously named, you don't call out to the woman by calling the child's name, do you?

Having the Spirit of God in you is like another dimension and can be compared to a pregnant woman carrying a child. However, this is regarding the spiritual realm.

People that don't have the Spirit of God within; are unable to know Christ or the Father and cannot differentiate between the two. Unable to realize the Father is a separate entity residing in Christ, they deny both the Father and Son's existence, revealing they are the Antichrist.

Not believing in spirits when ***God is a spirit, Jn 4:24.*** Yet deceived by Satan, an evil spirit.

Now Scripture only touches on the fact that Satan used to be a beautiful angel in heaven. As Christ said, ***I beheld Satan as lightning fall from heaven, Lk 10:18.*** The Devil caused an insurgency in heaven. Cast unto the earth, the world became the prison for Satan and his cohorts.

Scripture informs us after Satan's fall 'the Lord told Satan, "***How have you fallen from heaven, O Lucifer, son of the morning!". how art thou cut down to the ground, which didst weaken the nations! For thou hast said in thine heart, I will ascend into heaven, I will exalt my throne above the stars of God: I will sit also upon the mount of the congregation, in the sides of the north: I will ascend above the heights of the clouds; I will be like the most High Isa 14: 12-14.*** x

We do not know what Satan did in heaven, but I am sure it was pretty horrific. The only sure thing is when a person is ***proud, they can become contentious***, as Proverbs thirteen, verse ten explains. And the word pride in this context means the epitome of conceit. Or that meaning arrogance without measure.

Verily what all scriptures show us is once Satan and his followers were cast unto earth and stripped of their celestial bodies. They went about as evil spirits to influence people and were the ruination of this world. Even to the point, they use humankind and believe they can take on all of heaven. ***And I saw the beast, and the kings of the earth, and their armies, gathered together to make war against him that sat on the horse, and against his army, Rv 19:19-20.***

The Reason God Created Mankind

The next chapter addresses the question of why God created humankind.

Thus saith the Lord, the Holy One of Israel, and his Maker, Ask me of things to come concerning my sons, and concerning the work of my hands command ye me. I have made the earth, and created man upon it: I, even my hands, have stretched out the heavens, and all their host have I commanded Isaiah 45: 11,12

I will go before thee, and make the crooked places straight: I will break in pieces the gates of brass, and cut in sunder the bars of iron: And I will give thee the treasures of darkness, and hidden riches of secret places, that thou mayest know that I, the Lord, which call thee by thy name, am the God of Israel, Isaiah 45: 2,3.

I have made the earth, and created man upon it: I, even my hands, have stretched out the heavens, and all their host have I commanded, Isaiah 45:12.

For thus saith the Lord that created the heavens; God himself that formed the earth and made it; he hath established it, he created it not in vain, he formed it to be inhabited: I am the Lord; and there is none else, Isaiah 45:18

So, Christ, by way of God [his maker], created the world, yet it was not in vain. Thereby, we know there had to have been a reason.

Written, ***Thou art worthy, O Lord, to receive glory and honour and power: for thou hast created all things, and for thy pleasure they are and were created, Rv 4:11.***

And because of this one verse, many people assume we are like toys you make for kids. They think when you succeed in life, this is for God's pleasure. And the rest of the population is doomed?

Proving this type of theology is taught by a proud person. Titus mentions ***there are many unruly and vain talkers, Titus 1:10.*** Whereas we find a story, Christ said in Luke sixteen, verses nineteen through twenty-three. The story is about a rich man who had plenty of goods stored up while a beggar named Lazarus lay at his gate, full of sores. The beggar desired the crumbs which fell from the rich man's table: moreover, the dogs came and licked his sores. Both men died, and the rich man went to hell while the Lord brought Lazarus to heaven.

Obviously, God does not get pleasure from people suffering, and it is for this reason we know God didn't create humankind like some wind-up toy.

To understand why God created humans, you need to know that there are captains, sergeants, and other officers in a great army. However, the portion of the Spirit that is in

Christ makes Christ the Commander in Chief, as explained in First Corinthians eleven, chapter three.

Christ, the Commander in Chief, explains how the Kingdom of God is fashioned using a military phrase. However, I want you to know that our warfare weapons are not carnal, so unlike those of this world, we don't have guns and munitions like others deem necessary. For you see, ***Wisdom is better than weapons of war, Ecl 9:18.***

And ***the word of God is quick, and powerful, and sharper than any twoedged sword, piercing even to the dividing asunder of soul and spirit, and of the joints and marrow, and is a discerner of the thoughts and intents of the heart, Heb 4:12.***

(For the weapons of our warfare are not carnal, but mighty through God to the pulling down of strong holds;), 2 Cor 10:4.

So you see, like the governments on earth, in heaven, we also have a chain of command. Yet like Christ said: ***But to sit on my right hand and on my left hand is not mine to give; but it shall be given to them for whom it is prepared, Mk 10:40.***

The Lord-God created the world when Satan disagreed with our commander in chief, which is Christ. It appears Satan wanted to take Christ's position. At which point, the devil and his renegade angels wanted to take heaven by storm. They disagreed with God's politics and rule and started a revolution.

At that time, the Holy Spirit resided in the angels of heaven, and their disobedience grieved the Holy Spirit that was in them. And to fully understand how God's Holy Spirit can inhabit a disobedient person and leave that person. All you have to do is read the story of King Saul.

How the story of King Saul went was when Israel was still fighting the nations around them. They also wanted to be like other nations and have a monarchy.

In those days, King Saul served the Lord, insomuch he was blessed by the Lord, and the Holy Spirit entered into Saul.

There was some skirmish going on, and Samuel, the prophet, commanded Saul to wait upon the Lord. Samuel was running late, and Saul wanted the adoration of people more than God. Not having faith, neither trusting what the Lord commanded him to do, Saul became impatient and decided to do things his way. At which point, ***the Spirit of the Lord departed from Saul, and an evil spirit from the Lord troubled him, 1 Sam 16: 14.*** The entire story can be read in first Samuel chapters thirteen through sixteen.

Another story in the New Testament explains how a person can be turned over to Satan and have the Spirit of God depart from them. It was when the apostles established the true Church. On that day, everyone pitched their money in, and it was divided among all where no one lacked for anything.

What took place is, ***Ananias, with Sapphira his wife, sold a possession, And kept back part of the price, his wife***

also being privy to it, and brought a certain part, and laid it at the apostles' feet, Acts 5: 1,2.

But Peter said, ***Ananias, why hath Satan filled thine heart to lie to the Holy Ghost, and to keep back part of the price of the land? Whiles it remained, was it not thine own? and after it was sold, was it not in thine own power? why hast thou conceived this thing in thine heart? thou hast not lied unto men, but unto God, Acts 5:3,4.***

And Ananias hearing these words fell down, and gave up the ghost: and great fear came on all them that heard these things, Acts 5:5.

Then Peter approached the man's wife, and said unto her, ***How is it that ye have agreed together to tempt the Spirit of the Lord? behold, the feet of them which have buried thy husband are at the door, and shall carry thee out. Then fell she down straightway at his feet, and yielded up the ghost: and the young men came in, and found her dead, and, carrying her forth, buried her by her husband, Acts 5: 9,10.***

Carried to their graves, the Spirit of God departed out of them. Whereas Ananias and his wife lost their souls, and God's spirit departed these deceitful people. Remember, death is to lose your body and suffer separation from God's Holy Spirit.

Paul told the Church when a person seeks to do evil to hand this person over to Satan. And the way this was explained in Scripture was during a time it was, ***reported***

commonly that there is fornication among you, and such fornication as is not so much as named among the Gentiles, that one should have his father's wife, 1 Cor 5:1.

He stated how the Church was puffed up and didn't mourn this behavior, ***1 Cor 5:1-2.***

At which point he said: ***For I verily, as absent in body, but present in spirit, have judged already, as though I were present, concerning him that hath so done this deed, In the name of our Lord Jesus Christ, when ye are gathered together, and my spirit, with the power of our Lord Jesus Christ, 1 Cor 5: 3, 4.***

If evil is found in a person, Paul said: ***To deliver this person over to Satan for the destruction of the flesh, that the spirit may be saved in the day of the Lord Jesus, 1 Cor 5:5.*** So the Holy Spirit could be returned unto the Lord. Don't you realize, people who follow Satan's deeds will in no way get into God's Kingdom?

I mean, what theology do you believe? After all, ***God spared not the angels that sinned, but cast them down to hell, and delivered them into chains of darkness, Pt 2:4.*** So why would a man think he is greater than the angels of heaven? Or why would God love you more than the angels of heaven?

And understanding how God's Spirit can leave a soul is important to understand. Because prior to war breaking out in heaven, God's Spirit was in these disobedient angels. Once revolt in heaven ensued; there ***was war in heaven:***

Michael and his angels fought against the dragon, and the dragon fought and his angels. And prevailed not; neither was their place found any more in heaven. And the great dragon was cast out, that old serpent, called the devil, and Satan, which deceives the whole world: he was cast out into the earth, and his angels were cast out with him, Rv 12: 7-9.

War taking place in heaven, these evil beings were captured and the Lord created the world.

At which point the Lord-God also created ***living creatures that hath life, and foul that may fly above the earth in the opening ferment of heaven, And God created every creature that moves, Gn 1:20.*** The opening firmament of heaven sounds like the heavens and earth were still in agitation and growth. And apparently, it was at this time the dinosaurs were created. We call them dinosaurs, but obviously, the Bible refers to them as dragons.

The obedient angels of heaven captured these disobedient beings and cast them unto the earth. Upon earth, they didn't have fruit from the tree of life, like the tree growing in Eden and found in heaven, Rv 22:2. Thereby, their glorious bodies could not sustain life, and they too turned into dust.

At which point, the Holy Spirit that had been in them returned to heaven. But the souls of these renegades, which Christ referred to as worms were like a bacterium unable to rest. And they began their journey; ***of going to and fro in the earth, walking up and down in it, Job 1:7.*** Thereby as ***an unclean spirit walketh through dry places, seeking rest, and finds none, Mt 12:43, Lk 11:24.***

Having insomnia and seeking rest, they inhabited these fantastic beasts, the dinosaurs—kind of like when Satan entered a heard of swine after Christ cast him out of a man. Or like the devil inhabited a serpent when he deceived Eve. And this is the reason in Revelation; this evil spirit earned the nickname of a snake, a great dragon, and a beast.

How the dinosaurs were destroyed is not recorded as no one was made privy to this. Nonetheless, dinosaurs became a stumbling block as they caused many to disbelieve in the Lord and our God.

However, we know once these beasts were annihilated, the Lord God created humankind upon the earth and not again angels in heaven.

The world then became the court where God tries the human soul.

Christ referred to this as the ***regeneration*** in Matthew nineteen as the Kingdom of God was being made new. Due to the Lord-God began drafting people into his kingdom. However, ***strait is the gate, and narrow is the way, which leadeth unto life, and few there be that find it, Mt 7:14.***

On top of that, ***if the righteous scarcely be saved, where shall the ungodly and the sinner appear, 1 Pt 4:18?***

Yet this is the reason God created humankind because the Lord God knew ***The heart is deceitful above all things, and desperately wicked: who can know it, Jer 17:9?***

Thereby, the hearts of individuals had to be tested. The Lord wasn't able to determine what would motivate a person given a free will. Sure, the works of God are marvelous. As explained, all of us have a brain so we can think and can calculate things. All of us have eyes to see, ears to hear, etc. However, love, greed, covetousness, stubbornness, deceit, and hate are emotions governed by a person's personality.

I suppose this is the difference in creating humans with a free will compared to creating robots. Yet and still if mankind created AI in a robot and this artificial intelligence turned on humans. What would they do?

So when the Garden of Eden was established, and a man chosen, he was placed in the garden to tend it. The tree of knowledge in the garden was to test Adam and Eve and see what motivated them.

And once Satan deceived Adam and Eve, he set about with his diabolic scheme to use humankind to overtake this world.

Then as the world progressed and was coming near its close, the Lord new the Roman Empire was about to come into play. And before the Empire could take hold, the Lord ***laid hold on the dragon, that old serpent, which is the devil, and Satan, and bound him a thousand years, Rv 20:2.***

Satan in the pit didn't mean sin was removed but prevented him from influencing humankind. The world not controlled by Satan kept society from progressing to fast in technology, whereby creating weapons of mass destruction was put on a back burner. Thereby Satan was cast ***into the bottomless pit, and shut him up, and set a seal upon him, that he should deceive the nations no more, till the thousand years should be fulfilled: and after that he must be loosed a little season, Rv 20:3.***

When Satan was captured and put into the pit, it was approximately a thousand years before Christ came: as Scripture shows us when this came about. This event is recorded when there came a day when Daniel was sitting by the river's side, Hiddekel.

Daniel was having dreams during those days and was perplexed as to what his dreams meant. While fasting and in prayer, this angel appeared unto him.

What Daniel told us is when he looked***, and behold a certain man clothed in linen, whose loins were girded with fine gold of Uphaz, Dn 10:5.*** And this man was also an angel dressed in shiny clothes—kind of like the one standing by Christ grave after he rose.

The angel told Daniel to: ***"Fear not: for from the first day that thou didst set thine heart to understand, and to chasten thyself before thy God, thy words were heard, and I am come for thy words. But the prince of the kingdom of Persia withstood me one and twenty days: but, lo, Michael, one of the chief princes, came to help me, Dn 10:***

12,13." Thereby revealing, Satan inhabited Persia's king. However, Revelation revealed when he was captured, Satan was imprisoned in the bottomless pit at that time.

I know the scoffers will say if God couldn't tell what motivated a person's heart, how did he know what the Roman Empire would do? I guess you have to know that God is light and in heaven, which allows him to see in the future. In other words, we can see a star in heaven, which is no longer there. But the star can look upon us while we are in the future.

Given a free will, the Lord-God was able to see how we would behave. Because once created, the Lord was able to view us in the future. Thereby He knows us before we are even born.

Nonetheless, ***God so loved the world, that he gave his only begotten Son, that whosoever believeth in him should not perish, but have everlasting life. Jn 3:16.*** It was never his goal for humans to follow in Satan's path. So, unlike the days of Noah or Lot, whereby God just destroyed a city, He sent his only begotten Son to explain the reason this world was going to be annihilated. Never to be rebuilt again like the days of Noah and Lot.

And like he told Jonah, ***"Should not I spare Nineveh, that great city, wherein are more than sixscore thousand persons that cannot discern between their right hand and their left hand; and also much cattle Jonah, 4:11?*** At which point, Christ coming told us everything the Lord expected. Whereby Christ said, ***"If I had not come and***

spoken unto them, they had not had sin: but now they have no cloke for their sin, Jn 15:22."

Then once Christ was born, before he began preaching the gospel, he went into the wilderness where he too would be tempted by the devil. (can you imagine the devil able to entice God? Where would that leave anyone?)

In any case, it was at that point, Satan took ***him up into a high mountain, shewed unto him all the kingdoms of the world in a moment of time. And the devil said unto him, all this power will I give thee, and the glory of them: for that is delivered unto me; and to whomsoever I will I give it. If thou therefore wilt worship me, all shall be thine, Lk 4: 5-7.***

Of course, Christ refused

Thereby a loud voice sounded in heaven saying, ***Now is come salvation, and strength, and the kingdom of our God, and the power of his Christ: for the accuser of our brethren is cast down, which accused them before our God day and night, Rv 12:10.***

Christ refused, yet we know there will be a man of sin who will not refuse. And this evil maniac of a spirit will possess him. This man will be a king or president, and he will influence the entire world.

THE BOTTOM LINE

Wisdom... ***The Lord possessed me in the beginning of his way, before his works of old, Proverbs 8:22.*** Of course, ***wisdom is justified of all her children Lk 7:35.***

Humanity has always been given a free will and has always been able to choose what they want to believe. Those who are fair and honest will do and believe good and honest things. Those who are dishonest will not. Neither how I judge but what Christ taught in Luke eight, chapter fifteen.

What is essential to understand is the Lord God didn't want another war in heaven, as Satan had caused. And this is why He created humanity on earth and not again beings [angels] in heaven.

The best I can make out is God's Spirit is lonesome without a soul, and the soul can be lonely without the Spirit. Thereby humans were made for God's pleasure, enabling the kingdom of God to be made new.

And of a truth, ***God so loved the world, that he gave his only begotten Son, that whosoever believeth in him should not perish, but have everlasting life, Jn 3:16.***

Everything Christ required is written in Matthew, Mark, Luke, and John. And Christ said, ***"If ye love me, keep my commandments Jn 14:15."***

So, the question is not; does God love you? The question is, do you love him?

PART 2

CHAPTER 1

OMEGA

WILL THERE BE ANY FAITH?

I am not a religious organization, nor can I tell you to go here or go there as I have no altar to walk down. For I only come in the name of the Lord and can say to you HE IS, and it is him you have to believe.

In the previous chapters, we have looked at the war Satan started, why God created the world, and why it was a narrow gate into the Kingdom of God.

Also, Christ revealed when this was made known, "***There will be weeping, and gnashing of teeth, when you see Abraham, Isaac and Jacob and all the prophets in the kingdom of God, but you yourselves thrust out Lk 13:28.***" Telling us once the Lord adequately established the kingdom of God, there would be great tribulation.

The tribulation is similar to the spanking of a child. After all, those in heaven created all people. And who has a child you don't correct when they have done wrong? When you correct a child, it is because you love them. Right? So I genuinely hope you hear. "***But if ye be without chastisement, whereof all are partakers, then are ye bastards, and not sons, Heb 12:8.***"

And because ***nothing is secret, that shall not be made manifest; neither any thing hid, that shall not be known and come abroad, Lk 8:17.*** Christ prayed for those who refused his doctrine. And because God is love and for the world's sake, the Lord will prove who has told the truth. This book's goal is; my hope it will give eyes to see and ears to hear. And I realize truth can be a little bit weirder than science-fiction.

However, Scripture tells us at the end of this world; there will be a new world. The world we inhabit now will pass away in a ball of flames never to rise again. Yet it is promised *there shall be,* ***a new heaven and a new earth: for the first heaven and the first earth were passed away; and there was no more sea, Rv 21:1.*** Sure, the gate into God's Kingdom was narrow, and our Lord wished all would have sought to enter therein but for reasons revealed were unable to.

Yet and still, because God is love and forgiving. Hence we know the reason John ***saw as it were a sea of glass***

mingled with fire: and them that had gotten the victory over the beast, and over his image, and over his mark, and over the number of his name, stand on the sea of glass, having the harps of God, Rv 15:2. Thereby many will come through this great tribulation and be saved.

The people saved would consist of ***a great multitude, which no man could number, of all nations, and kindreds, and people, and tongues, stood before the throne, and before the Lamb, clothed with white robes, and palms in their hands, Rv 7:9.***

And there shall be a great cry, ***saying, Salvation to our God which sitteth upon the throne, and unto the Lamb, Rv 7:10.***

And all the angels stood round about the throne, and about the elders and the four beasts, fell before the throne on their faces, and worshipped God, Rv 7:11.

Saying, Amen: Blessing, and glory, and wisdom, and thanksgiving, and honor, and power, and might, be unto our God for ever and ever. Amen, Rv 7:12.

And one of the elders answered, saying unto me, What are these which are arrayed in white robes? and whence came they, Rv 7:13?

And I said unto him, Sir, thou knowest. And he said to me, These are they which came out of great tribulation, and have washed their robes, and made them white in the blood of the Lamb, Rv 7:14.

Therefore are they before the throne of God, and serve him day and night in his temple: and he that sitteth on the throne shall dwell among them, Rv 7:15.

They shall hunger no more, neither thirst anymore; neither shall the sun light on them, nor any heat, Rv 7:16.

And I saw as it were a sea of glass mingled with fire: and them that had gotten the victory over the beast, and over his image, and over his mark, and over the number of his name, stand on the sea of glass, having the harps of God, Rv 15:2.

And they sing the song of Moses the servant of God, and the song of the Lamb, saying, Great and marvelous are thy works, Lord God Almighty; just and true are thy ways, thou King of saints, Rv 15:3.

Who shall not fear thee, O Lord, and glorify thy name? for thou only art holy: for all nations shall come and worship before thee; for thy judgments are made manifest, Rv 15:4

And in this new world, we find, "***The wolf also shall dwell with the lamb, The leopard shall lie down with the young goat, The calf and the young lion and the fatling together; And a little child shall lead them, Isa 11:6.***"

And the cow and the bear shall feed; their young ones shall lie down together: and the lion shall eat straw like the ox, Isa 11:7.

And the sucking child shall play on the hole of the asp, and the weaned child shall put his hand on the cockatrice' den, Isa 11:.8.

They shall not hurt nor destroy in all my holy mountain: for the earth shall be full of the knowledge of the Lord, as the waters cover the sea, Isa 11:9.

Plus, we find in the kingdom of Heaven ***"In the midst of the street of it, and on either side of the river, was there the tree of life, which bare twelve manner of fruits, and yielded her fruit every month: and the leaves of the tree were for the healing of the nations, Rv 22:2."*** As Adam provided fruit to those outside of Eden's Garden, Heaven will provide fruit and healing to those saved.

Therefore, ***I saw another angel fly in the midst of heaven, having the everlasting gospel to preach unto them that dwell on the earth, and to every nation, and kindred, and tongue, and people. Saying with a loud voice, Fear God, and give glory to him; for the hour of his judgment is come: and worship him that made heaven, and earth, and the sea, and the fountains of waters, Rv 14:6, 7.***

And he that sat on the throne said, "Behold, I make all things new." And He said to me, "Write, for these words are true and faithful, Rv 21:5."

Heaven and the New World

We find God's Kingdom is in heaven, and the Kingdom of God will reign over the new earth. And it will be like their government.

To find the whereabouts of the new world and heaven, there is a fascinating story in second Corinthians twelve verses two and three. The apostle explained how he ***"knew a man in Christ above fourteen years ago, (whether in the body, I cannot tell; or whether out of the body, I cannot tell: God knoweth;) such an one caught up to the third heaven, 2 Cor 12:2".*** Paul didn't know if it were a vision this man had. Or if the Lord transported this man to heaven.

Regardless, we find the third heaven is apparently where the throne of God is. And that is what is essential to see in what Paul was telling us.

The we find another story, Christ told it was about a rich man and a beggar, we also can find the third heaven. And as the story was told follows:

There was a certain rich man, which was clothed in purple and fine linen, and fared sumptuously every day, Lk 16:19.

And there was a certain beggar named Lazarus, which was laid at his gate, full of sores, Lk 16:20.

And desiring to be fed with the crumbs which fell from the rich man's table: moreover the dogs came and licked his sores, Lk 16:21.

And it came to pass, that the beggar died, and was carried by the angels into Abraham's bosom: the rich man also died, and was buried, Lk 16: 22.

And in hell he lift up his eyes, being in torments, and seeth Abraham afar off, and Lazarus in his bosom, Lk 16:23.

And he cried and said, Father Abraham, have mercy on me, and send Lazarus, that he may dip the tip of his finger in water, and cool my tongue; for I am tormented in this flame, Lk 16: 24.

But Abraham said, Son, remember that thou in thy lifetime receivedst thy good things, and likewise Lazarus evil things: but now he is comforted, and thou art tormented, Lk 16:25.

And beside all this, between us and you there is a great gulf fixed: so that they which would pass from hence to you cannot; neither can they pass to us, that would come from thence, Lk 16:26.

Christ was speaking hypothetically, yet he mentions a gulf or a galaxy between those on earth (hell) and heaven. He calls the second heaven a great gulf. So, even in this story, there is our heaven, second heaven, and the third heaven which enables us to find the Kingdom of Heaven.

For you see, this world will be set on fire which is where we find hell.

And to understand what I am trying to show you in this story, I know a wormhole is a science fiction theory. But I believe it is real or something like it is. The reason is if you were to go into a wormhole, perhaps it would take you into another galaxy (A GREAT GULF) or that being the 2nd heaven. You would have to find another wormhole that would take you into another universe and the 3rd heaven. And this is where the throne of Christ and God is.

Now the Kingdom of God shall reign over the new world and will be like their government. It was a kingdom for the Jews, which was God's elect. And this was the reason Christ was sent to the Jews. And because there were some who didn't believe and trust in the Lord-God was anyone else able to join this magnificent administration.

Heaven will be like the sun shining its light upon the new earth. And how this is written ***"And the city had no need of the sun, neither of the moon, to shine in it: for the glory of God did lighten it, and the Lamb*** **is** ***the light thereof, Rv 21:23."***

Thereby, ***a great voice out of heaven saying, Behold, the tabernacle of God is with men, and he will dwell with them, and they shall be his people, and God himself shall be with them, and be their God, Rv 21:3.***

Third seal and Black Horse

And when he had opened the third seal, I heard the third beast say, Come and see. And I beheld, and lo a black horse; and he that sat on him had a pair of balances in his hand, Rv 6:5. The scale designates judgment when these movements (black horse) rise forth.

And the judgment brings in the beginning of tribulation whereby we find inflation as written: ***A measure of wheat for a penny, and three measures of barley for a penny; and see thou hurt not the oil and the wine, Rv 6:6.*** A penny in this passage is a day's wage.

And to find what this black horse is: In the United States and around the world, Black Lives Matter is a movement. They have been taught as youngsters that an injustice has been committed against them.

I haven't walked in anyone's shoes, and it is not for me to judge.

All I know is injustice was committed against Christ and the apostles, and they sure didn't make a spectacle of themselves, loot, cause riots, or burn down buildings.

Even Christ, when crucified, he requested the Father to forgive them. For you see, God is love, and He also forgives as long as you can forgive those who have done you wrong.

So has brutality, tyranny, repression, suppression, exploitation, bigotry, favoritism, partiality, one-sidedness, discrimination, partisanship, intolerance been done to these groups. I'm sure it has as I think we all have experienced this in one way or another.

Additionally, many Muslim groups like Al Queda, Taliban, and Al Shabaab dress all in black, flying black flags, claiming injustice has been committed against them. Some even become suicide killers. They have to think they are fighting for the good, and paradise awaits them.

Years ago, during WW II, the Japanese practiced Hari-Kari, where they too would commit suicide for the sake of their country and injustice committed unto them.

Nonetheless, and essential to understanding is murder is defined as one who takes another person's life, and Galatians five, starting at verse nineteen, explains a murderer will not inherit the Kingdom of God.

Christ was murdered and forgave them, and we know if a person repents, they can still be saved.

However, the thing to note is when you kill yourself, there is no way to regret or repent from it due to you are dead. And if God would judge a person for killing you and he didn't repent. He would judge him harshly. Thereby if you kill yourself, God has to judge you the same way because you would have killed the same person. Namely you! For you see, the God of heaven does not show favoritism; neither is He a hypocrite, as declared in Romans two verse eleven!

What about war? Don't people kill others in war? I know as explained before many will use the story of Daniel in Scripture as he was a man on the battlefield. And during the days of Daniel, they were fighting over real estate. However, if you had believed Christ who forewarned he was sent towards the end of this world to tell us what the Father wanted, you would have realized this world has since been given over to Satan.

And like revealed during the days of Nineveh after Lot told them of their judgment, they repented. God had empathy for the city because there was no-one to explain what the Lord-God wanted. Once they repented in old clothing and were remorseful, the Lord spared their city.

But since Christ explained what God expected, there are no more excuses. As Christ himself said, "***If I had not come and spoken unto them, they had not had sin: but now they have no cloke for their sin, Jn 15:22.***

And to choose this world and real estate over heaven is to be a friend of this world, thereby making you the enemy of God. As stated in James, ***Know ye not that the friendship of the world is enmity with God, Jms 4:4?*** Those in Christ strive to enter into heaven, and if we are ***mindful of that country from whence they came out, they might have had opportunity to have returned, Heb 15:15.*** If we consider our county and the continent born on, I suppose we would think of that as our home and not heaven.

Besides that, all countries believe they are right and will have their young men go to war and risk their lives. If their young men die, they all assume paradise awaits them. At which point, regardless of what country they fight for, their countrymen will praise them. Don't you see it? ***We wrestle not against flesh and blood, but against principalities, against powers, against the rulers of the darkness of this world, against spiritual wickedness in high places, Eph 6:12.*** And like previously mentioned, didn't the Roman Empire fight for their country? Didn't the British Empire do the same? Yet where are they now?

If you can comprehend and hear what the Spirit says, there is but one great commandment, and ***thou shalt love the Lord thy God with all thy heart, and with all thy soul, and with all thy mind, and with all thy strength: this is the first commandment. And the second is like, namely this, Thou shalt love thy neighbour as thyself, Mk 12:30-31.*** And if there aren't any other commandments more significant than these, how can you go to war and claim to love your fellow man?

And yes, there is a lot of evil and injustice in this world. However, we follow Christ and know there is one who will judge. God has scheduled a time when he will bring judgment upon the entire world. Because the words that Christ proclaimed, they didn't believe. Christ said ***He that rejecteth me, and receiveth not my words, hath one that judgeth him: the word that I have spoken, the same shall judge him in the last day, Jn 12:48***. So, when I witness earthquakes, tsunamis, storms, fires, pandemics, volcanoes, etc. I am not so vain as to believe the Lord God needs my help.

CHAPTER 2

FORGIVENESS TAUGHT BY THE STORY OF JOSEPH

Christ also testified in Matthew fourteen, ***for if ye forgive men their trespasses, your heavenly Father will also forgive you: But if ye forgive not men their trespasses, neither will your Father forgive your trespasses, Mt 6:14.*** In other words, you have to be able to forgive people when they commit acts against you. If you can do this, then God will forgive you.

To forgive doesn't mean you riot in the streets, go to war, and sue others because you got sick after eating something, etc. How can you say you forgive others and take them to court and sue them? Or look at the division in all the countries. If you have a tender heart, why would you be prone to violence, war, rioting, and strife? Christ said unto us, ***that ye resist not evil: but whosoever shall smite thee on thy right cheek, turn to him the other also, Mt 5:39.***

Christ revealed the truth of forgiveness but Joseph a man sold in slavery also showed what was meant to have forgiving spirit.

Joseph's story is found in Genesis and is regarding Joseph; Whereas ***Israel loved Joseph more than all his children, because he was the son of his old age: and he made him a coat of many colors. And when his brethren saw that their father loved him more than all his brethren, they hated him, and could not speak peaceably unto him, Gn 37: 3, 4.***

One-night Joseph had a dream of becoming a monarch over the rest of his family. And the second night, Joseph had another similar dream. Reporting his dreams to his family caused his brothers to be envious, and because they were jealous, they hated him more.

One day his brothers were tending to the flock, and Joseph went out to meet them.

After finding where his brothers went, as they saw him approach, they conspired to kill him. However, once he arrived, they decided to throw him into a pit.

While they sat their eating lunch, a caravan came by on their way to Egypt. One of Joseph's brothers convinced them they shouldn't kill him but sell him to be a slave instead.

Held as a slave and thrown in prison. After some year passed, a string of events occurred wherein the Lord intervened, and Pharaoh made Joseph governor over the land of Egypt. Gn 42:7.

Because Joseph was capable of interpreting dreams, he was made privy to a famine that would come. The king put him in charge of storing up all the grain. Once the grievous famine hit Joseph's father sent his sons to Egypt to purchase some food.

Several years had passed, so when his brothers arrived in Egypt, they didn't recognize Joseph. And they appealed to the governor their brother and requested he give them food or they would perish.

Joseph recognized them, and after playing a couple of tricks on them. ***Then Joseph could not refrain himself before all them that stood by him; and he cried, Cause every man to go out from me. And there stood no man with him, while Joseph made himself known unto his brethren, Gn 45:1.*** Sending out the Egyptian guards and made himself known to his brothers

But what I want you to see is Joseph had no animosity towards them, but instead, moved his entire family to Egypt to care for them.

The next thing to see in this story, is when God chose Jacob who was Joseph father, the tribes of Israel were established. He had twelve sons, and each son's offspring became a tribe for the house of Israel. Yet only one of Jacob's sons showed compassion and had forgiveness. Whereby only Joseph showed love and integrity.

And the point of this story reveals that when Christ came, he chose twelve apostles, one for each tribe of Israel. And one apostle was a son of perdition. Thereby Christ said: ***"While I was with them in the world, I kept them in thy name: those that thou gavest me I have kept, and none of them is lost, but the son of perdition; that the scripture might be fulfilled, Jn 17:12."***

In other words, Christ on purpose chose an apostle that would sell him out because all of Jacob's sons failed except one, and that was Joseph. And like Judas sold out Christ, his brothers sold Joseph out because they were envious.

Thereby, we know in the kingdom of heaven Joseph's name is written in the walls of heaven with the other apostles, ***And the wall of the city had twelve foundations, and in them the names of the twelve apostles of the Lamb, Rv 21:14.***

- Andrew
- Simon Peter
- James Zebedee
- John Zebedee
- Philip
- Nathaniel
- Matthew Levi
- Thomas Didymus
- James and Judas Alpheus
- Simon the Zealot
- Joseph

Beloved, let us love one another: for love is of God; and every one that loveth is born of God, and knoweth God. He that loveth not knoweth not God; 1 Jn 4:7,8.

Yet, as Judas sold Christ for money, Joseph's brothers sold him. Whereby they lost their inheritance in the Kingdom of God. ***For many are called, but few are chosen Mt 22:14.*** Don't you see it? If the brothers of Joseph could fail, where does that leave you? ***For if ye forgive men their trespasses, your heavenly Father will also forgive you: But if ye forgive not men their trespasses, neither will your Father forgive your trespasses, Mt 6:14,15.***

"Love worketh no ill to his neighbour: therefore love is the fulfilling of the law. Rom 13:10"

WHAT ABOUT THE CHILDREN?

We know God is the Word, He is love, yet He cannot lie. In this chapter, we want to investigate if God is love, how could He destroy a world full of people, including children.

Christ explained the days of judgment would be like the days of Noah. ***For as in the days that were before the flood they were eating and drinking, marrying and giving in marriage, until the day that Noe entered into the ark Mth 24:38.*** If they were getting married, they had children. Right?

Christ coming will be like the days of Lot, and according to the stories in Scripture, they sure weren't celibate. So, they too were having children. Right?

Even the Old Testament explained when we reached the last days and the judgment***, even if Noah, Daniel, and Job were alive they would not be able to save a son nor daughter, but they would only be able to save their own souls by their own righteousness, Ezk 14:20.***

Second Peter explains how Noah's days unfolded wherein: ***The Lord spared not the old world, but saved Noah the eighth person, a preacher of righteousness, bringing in the flood upon the world of the ungodly 2 Pt 2:5.*** Telling us the Lord only saved Noah's soul.

Whereas, First Peter chapter explains ***there were few, that is, eight souls were saved by water 1 Pt 3:20.*** Eight people only were rescued from the floods, and no one else!

So, if God is love, and all things are possible for God except to lie! Then how would it have been possible for God to destroy all except Noah's soul from death, and only Noah's families from the flood, and killed the rest, even children?

The Lord destroying children, casting out angels, and yet he is love, and forgiving can be a perplexing puzzle.

Yet we find, ***The beginning of wisdom is to fear the Lord*** because you know he is not a liar, Prv 9:10. Additionally, all of Scripture reveals, ***It is a fearful thing to fall into the hands of the living God Heb 10:31.***

For if God spared not the angels that sinned, but cast them down to hell, and delivered them into chains of darkness, to be reserved unto judgment; 2 Pt 2:4. By this, I would say I don't think God plays.

And spared not the old world, but saved Noah the eighth person, a preacher of righteousness, bringing in the flood upon the world of the ungodly; 2 Pt 2:5. So again I asked myself what about the children?

And turning the cities of Sodom and Gomorrha into ashes condemned them with an overthrow, making them an ensample unto those that after should live ungodly; 2 Pt 2:6 That was also reported in Second Peter and don't you think they had children too?

So, what happens to the children? And to find out, we will again search all of Scripture.

First, we know the soul belongs to God, and children are but a loan unto us. If a soul goes to heaven or hell, it belongs to God.

Two thousand years ago, when Christ lived amongst us on earth, he said, ***now is the judgment of this world: now shall the prince of this world be cast out, Jn 21:31.*** In other words, the beginning of God's Judgment came when Jesus came. During that day, like today, the religions had deceived many people.

Pretentious, we know these false apostles shall not be established in God's kingdom. And the reason is they set themselves up and were not a chosen vessel of the Lords. ***For when they speak great swelling words of vanity, they allure through the lusts of the flesh, through much wantonness, those that were clean escaped from them who live in error 2 Pt 2:18 While they promise them liberty, they themselves are the servants of corruption: 2 Pt 2:29.***

These false apostles, not understanding Scripture, think they can hide behind the children. As they know, God is love and forgiving, which has caused them to use children for their means.

So, to find the reason the Lord can judge the entire world, including children, is because He gives every soul a chance.

The New Testament explains it this way when we are told, ***"it is appointed unto men once to die, but after this***

the judgment, Heb 9:27." Doesn't this verse mean we live one time, die, and then are brought back unto the judgment? Yet Christ said now is the judgment?

So to investigate how this can happen, we find when those of apostate faiths crucified, Christ. Those who died believing in Christ during that day rose from the dead. The way this is told in Scripture is: ***"the veil of the temple was rent in twain from the top to the bottom; the earth did quake, and the rocks rent; Mt 27:51. And the graves were opened; and many bodies of the saints which slept arose, Mt 27:52. And came out of the graves after his resurrection, and went into the holy city, and appeared unto many, Mt 27:53.***

So those who lived during the days of Christ, died once, but were immediately resurrected unto the day of judgment. Remember, Christ brought in the day of judgment.

Those that believe in Christ are not brought back unto condemnation. But it was proving the day of judgment had come. As the apostle explained, ***it is appointed unto men once to die, but after this the judgment, Heb 9:27.*** So those in Christ died one time and were brought back unto the day of judgment.

Christ also proved this to be true in another story written in John, whereby Lazarus had died, and Jesus said unto his disciples, ***Lazarus is dead, Jn 11:14. And I am glad for your sake that I was not there, to the intent ye may believe; nevertheless, let us go unto him, Jn 11:15. Then said Thomas, which is called Didymus, unto his*** *fellow disciples, Let us also go, that we may die with him, Jn 11:16. Then when Jesus came, he found that he had laid in the grave four days already, Jn 11:17.*

Now Bethany was nigh unto Jerusalem, about fifteen furlongs off: Jn 11:18.

And many of the Jews came to Martha and Mary, to comfort them concerning their brother. Then Martha, as soon as she heard that Jesus was coming, went and met him: but Mary sat still in the house. Then said Martha unto Jesus, Lord, if thou hadst been here, my brother had not died, Jn 11:19-21.

But I know, that even now, whatsoever thou wilt ask of God, God will give it thee. Jesus saith unto her, Thy brother shall rise again. Martha saith unto him, I know that he shall rise again in the resurrection at the last day. Jesus said unto her, I am the resurrection, and the life: he that believe's in me, though he were dead, yet shall he live: And whosoever lives and believes in me shall never die. Believest thou this, Jn 11:22- 26?

She saith unto him, Yea, Lord: I believe that thou art the Christ, the Son of God, which should come into the world. And when she had so said, she went her way, and called Mary her sister secretly, saying, The Master is come, and calls for thee. As soon as she heard that, she arose quickly, and came unto him, Jn 11:26-29.

Now Jesus was not yet come into the town, but was in that place where Martha met him Jn 11: 30

The Jews then which were with her in the house, and comforted her, when they saw Mary, that she rose up hastily and went out, followed her, saying, She went unto the grave to weep there, Jn 11:31.

Then when Mary was come where Jesus was, and saw him, she fell down at his feet, saying unto him, Lord, if thou hadst been here, my brother had not died, Jn 11:32.

When Jesus therefore saw her weeping, and the Jews also weeping which came with her, he groaned in the spirit, and was troubled. And said, where have ye laid him? They said unto him, Lord, come and see. Jesus wept, Jn 11:33-35.

Then said the Jews, behold how he loved him! And some of them said, could not this man, which opened the eyes of the blind, have caused that even this man should not have died, Jn 11:36-37?

Jesus therefore again groaning in himself went to the grave. It was a cave, and a stone lay upon it, Jn 11:38.

Jesus said, Take ye away the stone. Martha, the sister of him that was dead, saith unto him, Lord, by this time he stinks: for he hath been dead four days. Jesus saith unto her, Said I not unto thee, that, if thou would believe, thou should see the glory of God, Jn 11:39-40?

Then they took away the stone from the place where the dead was laid. And Jesus lifted up his eyes, and said, Father, I thank thee that thou hast heard me. And I

knew that thou hear me always: but because of the people which stand by I said it, that they may believe that thou hast sent me. And when he thus had spoken, he cried with a loud voice, Lazarus, come forth, Jn 11: 41-43.

And he that was dead came forth, bound hand and foot with grave clothes: and his face was bound about with a napkin. Jesus saith unto them, loose him, and let him go, Jn 11:44.

As Jesus testified, the day of judgment had arrived. Whereby, Lazarus too, died and was brought back. This was because the day Christ walked upon earth he brought in the day of judgment.

Of course, those in Christ don't die a ***second death, Rv 20:14***. This is because the second death has no power over those who believe him.

Revelation twenty, verse fourteen, explains ***that the second death*** is not meant to harm those who have ears to hear and comprehend what Christ taught. Because when you believe in the God who sent Christ, you shall not come into condemnation, which is explained in John five, verse twenty-four.

And because they are not brought into condemnation when the great tribulation hits, they are not cast into tribulation with others. They are not taken out of the world but in a sense enter the ark. For you see, ***The kingdom of heaven is like to a grain of mustard seed, which a man took, and sowed in his field: Which indeed is the least of***

all seeds: but when it is grown, it is the greatest among herbs, and becometh a tree, so that the birds of the air come and lodge in the branches thereof Mt 13:14, 15.

So I hope you see why Christ explained, ***"The hour is coming, and now is, when the dead shall hear the voice of the Son of God: and they that hear shall live, Jn 5:25."*** In other words when Christ walked upon earth some people had previously died while others were born in other parts of the world. And these would be reincarnated during a time they would have a chance to hear God's Word.

To enable Christ's voice to be heard worldwide was the reason the gospel had to be published in all nations, Mk 13:10.

If reincarnated, you would have died once and are brought back unto the day of judgment.

Whereby if a person died as a child in their first life and had never heard of Christ or what he taught, he would be brought back and given a chance to grow up in his next life. At which point, men directed by God published the Bible. Providing all a chance to hear the Lord's words.

Others may have lived in other parts of the world in their first life and never had a chance to hear his word and they too are brought back and given an opportunity once the Bible was published.

Of course, if they didn't have a good and honest heart, reject and refuse to believe what Christ taught, then they will stand in judgment when reincarnated. And many of such will go through great tribulation as explained.

And because the high priest would be reincarnated Christ told him in Mark fourteen, verse sixty-two that he would see Jesus "***sitting at the right hand of the Power, and coming with the clouds of heaven, Mk 14:62."*** Christ sitting on the right hand of God means Christ is God's number one man. Just as you use your right hand for all things, Christ is the person God uses. Thereby, we know when Jesus comes in God's power, the high priest and others shall be reincarnated and witness his coming.

Hence at the end of this judgment, it shall bring the day of the Lord. The gate into the Kingdom of God shall be closed, yet as revealed, Christ still prayed for those who didn't believe in him, saying***: "Father, forgive them; for they know not what they do," Lk 23:34.***

Many won't be granted a seat in the Kingdom of God but can perhaps inherit the new world if they repent.

We can see, in this day, some people are mentally gone and are unable to comprehend anything. But because I know God is good and God is love if a person lived a previous life and said despicable things towards God's Spirit. ***Wherefore I say unto you, All manner of sin and blasphemy shall be forgiven unto men: but the blasphemy against the Holy Ghost shall not be forgiven unto men, Mt 12:31.***

It's not for me to judge but to believe. I can't see a person's heart, and I know God is good and God is love.

And those who have chosen Satan will not sneak much less be coerced into anything.

Of course, those who chose Satan's spirit, causing others to worship him and called him their God, have chosen death. ***And death and hell were cast into the lake of fire. This is the second death, Rv 20:14.***

For you see, God is love, but He is not a liar. Nor does he show favoritism as He is not a respecter of persons. But he does give everyone a chance because ***there no salvation in any other: for there is none other name under heaven given among men, whereby we must be saved, Acts 4:12.***

CHAPTER 3

JUDGMENT

Cities are being destroyed, and because of their hearts' hardness, they rebuild and still fail to hear. God is good, and He, of course, gives a person time to repent. Remember, Cane's brother Able in Genesis of the Bible? How the Lord was gracious and even spared his life for a time. Nonetheless, it is essential not to run out of time, for ***it is a fearful thing to fall into the hands of the living God, Heb 10:32.***

People read Scripture and seem to think things will happen all in their lifetime. However, God is not on our timetable, and prophecy can take years if not hundreds of years to fulfill. Meaning you can read one sentence in the Bible, and that sentence may take a hundred years or more to complete.

So in a sense, this chapter is a history review and unraveling of prophecy. As even Revelation one verse four explains, it gives us information about things that are past, were happening, and some things were yet to come.

THE FOURTH SEAL

And when he had opened the fourth seal, I heard the voice of the fourth beast say, Come and see Rv 6:7

And I looked, and behold a pale horse: and the name that sat on him was Death, and Hell followed with him. And power was given unto them over the fourth part of the earth, to kill with sword, and with hunger, and with death, and with the beasts of the earth Rv 6:8.

The fourth seal opened we find war, famine, death as the day of the Lord comes like a thief and presents itself. Have we arrived there? It does appear that it is close.

BABYLON VS. MYSTERY BABYLON

According to Scripture, watching for the day of the Lord, and what I was contemplating was Babylon's story. And the reason I was thinking about this was Revelation also speaks of a great city mystery Babylon.

Originally Babylon in Genesis, when the inhabitants traveled and built a great city, they didn't find other people on their trip. Not seeing other people caused them to be perplexed. Confused, they wanted to leave a landmark for others if they got dispersed. So, they built huge buildings that reached unto heaven. We can find buildings like this in this day.

Today, people do not understand why God created humankind, so; they look for life on other planets. Not believing God, they, too, cannot fathom that they are the only lifeforms created. And they also want to leave a footprint and have left a flag on the moon, build rovers, etc.

Not having faith in God is how this evil spirit uses people to try and climb into heaven.

The difference between Babylon in Genesis and mother Babylon in Revelation is Mother Babylon sits on a beast with seven mountains for heads. We know a mountain coming out of the see is a continent. Thereby, this woman, by way of an evil spirit, deceives and sits upon the entire world.

If you recall, sorcery is to copy many of God's accomplishments. Munitions of mass destruction, cloning animals, etc.

Thereby to find the judgment of this world, it will be necessary to understand where the bottomless pit is.

Bottomless Pit

First of all, Scripture explains this evil spirit ***the beast that thou sawest was, and is not; and shall ascend out of the bottomless pit, and go into perdition, Rv 17:8:***

As revealed in a previous chapter, the angel captured this evil spirit and bound him in the bottomless pit. Held captive for a thousand years and released, he marched forward to overtake the world.

To find the bottomless pit and where Satan was held captive. We know our galaxy has no beginning or end, and it is bottomless.

Scripture then reveals Satan released from the pit, appeared as a star falling from heaven. Whereas ***the fifth angel sounded, and I saw a star fall from heaven unto the earth: and to him was given the key of the bottomless pit, Rv 9:1.*** The key to the bottomless pit represents access to knowledge regarding the bottomless pit's mysteries. And if our heavens are where we find the bottomless pit, then the mysteries of heaven are unraveled.

And when ***he opened the bottomless pit; and there arose a smoke out of the pit, as the smoke of a great furnace; and the sun and the air were darkened by reason of the smoke of the pit, Rv 9:2.*** Telling us once the bottomless pit and its mysteries unraveled, smoke arises like a vast furnace burning. We have fires burning in the United States and other parts of the world. Air currents carry the smoke over thousands and thousands of miles.

The Judgment of Babylon the Great

A day of darkness and of gloominess, a day of clouds and of thick darkness, as the morning spread upon the mountains: a great people and a strong; there hath not been ever the like, neither shall be any more after it, even to the years of many generations, Joel 2:2.

Reading Joel, chapter two, it appears when God's army marches forward this judgment is also written in Revelation. Whereby, ***A fire devoureth before them; and behind them a flame burneth: the land is as the garden of Eden before them, and behind them a desolate wilderness; yea, and nothing shall escape them, Joel 2: 3.*** So before them, the world is like a garden of Eden. And when this judgment marches forth nothing shall escape.

For then shall be great tribulation, such as was not since the beginning of the world to this time, no, nor ever shall be, Rv 24:21.

They overtook homes like thieves, the people's faces were pained. Joel 2:6. For as you have done unto others now shall it be done unto you. ***For with what judgment you judge, you will be judged; and with the measure you use, it will be measured back to you, Mt 7:2.***

And this evil spirit by way of man had deceived: ***them that dwell on the earth by the means of those miracles which he had power to do in the sight of the beast; saying to them that dwell on the earth, that they should make an image to the beast, which had the wound by a sword, and did live, Rv:13:14.***

The Roman Empire, deceived by an evil spirit, was the first beast, and its image would be a likeness. Thereby a city influenced by an evil spirit would rise. John saw the woman sitting on the beast and told us: ***the woman which thou sawest is that great city, which reigneth over the kings of the earth, Rv 17:18.***

And there came one of the seven angels which had the seven vials, and talked with me, saying unto me, Come hither; I will shew unto thee the judgment of the great whore that sitteth upon many waters, Rv 17:1:

With whom the kings of the earth have committed fornication, and the inhabitants of the earth have been made drunk with the wine of her fornication, Rv 17:2.

So he carried me away in the spirit into the wilderness: and I saw a woman sit upon a scarlet coloured beast, full of names of blasphemy, having seven heads and ten horn, Rv 17:3.

Eating the fruit from the tree of knowledge enabled this evil spirit via humans to gain the knowledge needed to open the secrets of heaven. Once the mysteries were unlocked, ***there came out of the smoke locusts upon the earth: and unto them was given power, as the scorpions of the earth have power, Rv 9:3.*** Does this mean out of the smoke and fires we see today, there will be another pestilence, bug, or virus that will eventually torment people? Or will this bug fall out of heaven? I viewed a video that showed life from the sky on meteorites are falling unto earth. https://www.youtube.com/watch?v=ZyXrtODhJEA

Regardless of how this bug or virus rises it shall: ***not hurt the grass of the earth, neither any green thing, neither any tree; but only those men which have not the seal of God in their foreheads, Rv 9:4.*** So this judgment appears to be upon those who are not sealed by God.

And to them it was given that they should not kill them, but that they should be tormented five months: and their torment was as the torment of a scorpion, when he striketh a man, Rv 9:5. Thereby, it's not COVID 19 as people can die from COVID-19. Plus, COVID has lasted longer than five months. So, are we about to see another pestilence? The judgment spoken of in Rv 9:5 will not cause people to die. However they may die from other things.

And in those days shall men seek death, and shall not find it; and shall desire to die, and death shall flee from them, Rv 9:6.

And the shapes of the locusts were like unto horses prepared unto battle; and on their heads were as it were crowns like gold, and their faces were as the faces of men, Rv 9:7.

And they had hair as the hair of women, and their teeth were as the teeth of lions, Rv 9:8.

And they had breastplates, as it were breastplates of iron; and the sound of their wings was as the sound of chariots of many horses running to battle, Rv 9:9.

And they had tails like unto scorpions, and there were stings in their tails: and their power was to hurt men five months, Rv 9:10.

And they had a king over them, which is the angel of the bottomless pit, whose name in the Hebrew tongue is Abaddon, but in the Greek tongue hath his name Apollyon, Rv 9:11. The first space missions were Appolo, again reveling the bottomless pit is our heavens and galaxy. Although there is another portion of the sky that is also named Appolo. Satan imprisoned in the bottomless pit was this pestilence contrived there too?

For thou hast said in thine heart, I will ascend into heaven, I will exalt my throne above the stars of God: I will sit also upon the mount of the congregation, in the sides of the north, Isa 14:13. I will ascend above the heights of the clouds; I will be like the most High, Isa 14:14.

And after these things I saw another angel come down from heaven, having great power; and the earth was lightened with his glory, Rv 18:1.

And he cried mightily with a strong voice, saying, Babylon the great is fallen, is fallen, and is become the

habitation of devils, and the hold of every foul spirit, and a cage of every unclean and hateful bird, Rv 18:2.

For all nations have drunk of the wine of the wrath of her fornication, and the kings of the earth have committed fornication with her, and the merchants of the earth are waxed rich through the abundance of her delicacies, Rv 18:3.

And I heard another voice from heaven, saying, Come out of her, my people, that ye be not partakers of her sins, and that ye receive not of her plagues, Rv 18:4.

For her sins have reached unto heaven, and God hath remembered her iniquities, Rv 18:5.

Reward her even as she rewarded you, and double unto her double according to her works: in the cup which she hath filled fill to her double, Rv 18:6.

How much she hath glorified herself, and lived deliciously, so much torment and sorrow give her: for she saith in her heart, I sit a queen, and am no widow, and shall see no sorrow, Rv 18:7.

Therefore shall her plagues come in one day, death, and mourning, and famine; and she shall be utterly burned with fire: for strong is the Lord God who judgeth her, Rv 18:8.

And the kings of the earth, who have committed fornication and lived deliciously with her, shall bewail her, and lament for her, when they shall see the smoke of her burning, Rv 18:9.

Standing afar off for the fear of her torment, saying, Alas, alas that great city Babylon, that mighty city! for in one hour is thy judgment come, Rv 18:10.

And the merchants of the earth shall weep and mourn over her; for no man buyeth their merchandise any more, Rv 18:11:

The merchandise of gold, and silver, and precious stones, and of pearls, and fine linen, and purple, and silk, and scarlet, and all thyine wood, and all manner vessels of ivory, and all manner vessels of most precious wood, and of brass, and iron, and marble, Rv 18:12.

And cinnamon, and odours, and ointments, and frankincense, and wine, and oil, and fine flour, and wheat, and beasts, and sheep, and horses, and chariots, and slaves, and souls of men, Rv 18:13.

And the fruits that thy soul lusted after are departed from thee, and all things which were dainty and goodly are departed from thee, and thou shalt find them no more at all, Rv 18:14.

The merchants of these things, which were made rich by her, shall stand afar off for the fear of her torment, weeping and wailing, Rv 18:15.

And saying, Alas, alas that great city, that was clothed in fine linen, and purple, and scarlet, and decked with gold, and precious stones, and pearls, Rv 18:16!

For in one hour so great riches is come to nought. And every shipmaster, and all the company in ships, and sailors, and as many as trade by sea, stood afar off, Rv 18:17.

And cried when they saw the smoke of her burning, saying, What city is like unto this great city, Rv 18:18!

And they cast dust on their heads, and cried, weeping and wailing, saying, Alas, alas that great city, wherein were made rich all that had ships in the sea by reason of her costliness! for in one hour is she made desolate, Rv 18:19.

Rejoice over her, thou heaven, and ye holy apostles and prophets; for God hath avenged you on her, Rv 18:20.

And a mighty angel took up a stone like a great millstone, and cast it into the sea, saying, Thus with violence shall that great city Babylon be thrown down, and shall be found no more at all, Rv 18:21.

And the voice of harpers, and musicians, and of pipers, and trumpeters, shall be heard no more at all in thee; and no craftsman, of whatsoever craft he be, shall be found any more in thee; and the sound of a millstone shall be heard no more at all in thee, Rv 18:22.

And the light of a candle shall shine no more at all in thee; and the voice of the bridegroom and of the bride shall be heard no more at all in thee: for thy merchants were the great men of the earth; for by thy sorceries were all nations deceived, Rv 18:23.

And in her was found the blood of prophets, and of saints, and of all that were slain upon the earth, Rv 18:24.

And by all of this, we have been able to find the Lord's Day, and it is near. And in that we find this pestilence or whatever it is will not touch the trees or grass. Yet***: the land is as the garden of Eden before them, and behind them a desolate wilderness.*** So apparently other judgments will arise and turn this world into a wilderness. In fact were kind of seeing it happen now with stores boarded up, streets full of trash, etc.

Repent

Therefore also now, saith the Lord, turn ye even to me with all your heart, and with fasting, and with weeping, and with mourning, Joel 2: 12:

And rend your heart, and not your garments, and turn unto the Lord your God: for he is gracious and merciful, slow to anger, and of great kindness, and repenteth him of the evil, Joel 2:13.

The Second woe

One woe is past; and, behold, there come two woes more hereafter, Rv 9:12

And the sixth angel sounded, and I heard a voice from the four horns of the golden altar which is before God, Rv 9:13.

Saying to the sixth angel which had the trumpet, Loose the four angels which are bound in the great river Euphrates, Rv 9:14.

And the four angels were loosed, which were prepared for an hour, and a day, and a month, and a year, for to slay the third part of men, Rv 9:15.

And the number of the army of the horsemen were two hundred thousand thousand: and I heard the number of them, Rv 9:16.

And thus I saw the horses in the vision, and them that sat on them, having breastplates of fire, and of jacinth, and brimstone: and the heads of the horses were as the heads of lions; and out of their mouths issued fire and smoke and brimstone, Rv 9:17.

By these three was the third part of men killed, by the fire, and by the smoke, and by the brimstone, which issued out of their mouths, Rv 9:18.

For their power is in their mouth, and in their tails: for their tails were like unto serpents, and had heads, and with them they do hurt, Rv 9:19.

And the rest of the men which were not killed by these plagues yet repented not of the works of their hands, that they should not worship devils, and idols of gold, and silver, and brass, and stone, and of wood: which neither can see, nor hear, nor walk, Rv 9:20:

SUMMARY OF CHAPTER

Realizing the beast is an evil spirit that deceives people. And Revelation revealed this creature has seven heads, which are mountains. The devil's goal was to deceive the entire world, and the world consists of seven continents.

The first power to reign over most of the world was the Roman Empire. History reveals the Roman Empire was the superpower of its day, boasting an army with the best training, most significant budgets, and equipment known to the world.

Ruled by an evil spirit, the Roman Empire killed and persecuted the church and reported to us in Acts twelve. During the time of Herod, ***the king stretched forth his hands to vex certain of the church. And he killed James the brother of John with the sword, Acts 12: 1, 2.***

And because he saw it pleased the Jews, he proceeded further to take Peter also. (Then were the days of unleavened bread.) And when he had apprehended him, he put him in prison, and delivered him to four

quaternions of soldiers to keep him; intending after Easter to bring him forth to the people, Acts 12: 3,4.

Then we discovered this brutal Empire known as a beast would suffer a head wound; the Roman Empire dissolved, whereby it was wounded unto death and faded away. Thereby, one continent or one of the beast's heads appeared dead.

The second beast arose and created an image of this animal. If you realize the first beast was a city possessed by an evil spirit, you would know a replica would be a city (Government) maintaining the same type of control the Roman Empire enjoyed.

The Roman Empire annihilated the church, and two branches that came out of her loins claimed they were the church. The two denominations are the protestant and catholic. They used Christ in name but didn't follow his teachings. Using Christ in name only refers to a religious harlot found sitting on this animal. ***And I saw the woman drunken with the blood of the saints, and with the blood of the martyrs of Jesus: and when I saw her, I wondered with great admiration, Rv*** **17:6.**

These apostate beliefs went to war, conquering new lands all in the name of their god. Even the United States was overtaken in this way. Not following what Christ taught but claiming they were like Daniel and were going to save the world, they slaughtered the native Indians in droves.

The years passed, times changed, and like a chameleon they portrayed themselves as the pursued and not the pursuer. The woman being apostate teachers sat on this beast, and she built a city whose people were possessed by evil spirits. She cunningly deceived all by flatteries. ***With whom the kings of the earth have committed fornication, and the inhabitants of the earth have been made drunk with the wine of her fornication, Rv 17:2.***

This woman is known as ***Mystery, Babylon The Great, The Mother Of Harlots And Abominations Of The Earth, Rv 17:5.***

At the end of the days, we find she will be granted three and a half years to continue. ***And there was given unto him a mouth speaking great things and blasphemies; and power was given unto him to continue forty and two months, Rv 13:5.***

Hence the Old World being the Roman Empire, faded away, and the New World being the United States rose from its ashes. For you see, the ***woman which thou sawest is that great city, which reigneth over the kings of the earth, Rv 17:18.***

HELL

Now Christ told us Satan and his followers would be captured alive and thrown into hell. We know Satan was arrested and thrown from heaven to earth. The sky caught on fire, and this world will be turned into a blazing fireball.

As written, the ***heavens shall pass away with a great noise, and the elements shall melt with fervent heat,***

the earth also and the works that are therein shall be burned up, Rv 9:10. Watching videos on YouTube, people are recording sounds coming from heaven. So is it closer than we realize?

This world set on fire is where we find Hell. ***And the beast was taken, and with him the false prophet that wrought miracles before him, with which he deceived them that had received the mark of the beast, and them that worshipped his image. These both were cast alive into a lake of fire burning with brimstone, Rv 19:20.***

But the heavens and the earth, which are now, by the same word are kept in store, reserved unto fire against the day of judgment and perdition of ungodly men. 2 Pt 3:7.

But, beloved, be not ignorant of this one thing, that one day is with the Lord as a thousand years, and a thousand years as one day, 2 Pt 3:8.

AUTHOR'S BIO

Reason I wrote this book

Scripture tells us when we talk about our accomplishments; it is because we are looking for fame and prestige from others. My goal has never been about me, but about what I was taught and who taught me.

First, I am a simple person and didn't graduate from any large college or have any exceptional degree. A simpleton, and I don't say that to appear humble but to tell you like it is. As First Corinthians one, verse twenty-seven tells us God chooses those that are silly and uneducated. That was me.

Like a child that believes in Santa when I read the Bible, I trust everything wholeheartedly. People in my life had failed me, and if I reached a point in my life if I couldn't trust God, there was no place else to go. And as for me, so as it was, then so is it now.

Trusting God to teach me Scripture as First John two, verse twenty-seven, tells us if we have received the Holy Spirit that proceeds from God, we have the teacher in us and don't need others to direct us. I believe what the Bible says and what I learned is what I have shared in this little book.

Neither have I written this little book for me, as I know beyond a shadow of a doubt that the Lord will prove who has told the truth. And if I have the facts and didn't share them, what kind of a person would I be?

So, to give you a little insight into who I am, I have written the following.

A SHORT BIO OF MY LIFE STORY

As a young girl, I had many emotional issues. Big for my age, it seemed everyone expected more from me. Or at least that is how I felt.

Having family problems, at twelve years old, I became a chronic runaway. On one of those escapades, I was picked up by a man who dropped me off on skid row. And unknowingly, I was about to have my life turned upside down as I was left where all the prostitutes, drug addicts, and pimps hung out. None of which I was at that time

I must have looked hungry to Bobby when he met me; he offered to buy me dinner. I, of course, took him up on his offer.

I don't recall how old I told him I was, but I sure didn't tell him I was a runaway. Nonetheless, if I ran into a young person who didn't have a change of clothes, money, or anything, I'm sure I'd know something was amiss, as I'm sure Bobby did. In any case, he took me under his wing, and I thought it was because he liked me.

I can't remember how long our romance lasted before the truth came out. Bobby wanted me to be a prostitute, and at first, I refused. As I mentioned, my family raised us with moral standards as a compass, even if we weren't a close-knit household.

Bobby would leave me if I didn't do as asked, and I had no one I could turn to, so I gave in to his demands. He told me it was to get ahead and didn't have anything to do with him, not loving me. Starved for love, I chose to believe his lies.

Bobby changed my name to Pat and directed me to call him daddy. He was twenty years older than me, and I thought he changed my name because we broke the law by me being a prostitute. But now realize it was to disguise who I was if the law was looking for a runaway as I'm sure he had to know.

And Like any con artist, they wine dine and make you feel special. I was hungry for love and wanted to love someone and have them love me. For many reasons at home, I didn't feel I had that.

Eventually, my life turned into a living hell. If I didn't make enough money, Bobby would beat; if I turned a trick for too little, daddy, as I called him, assaulted me, and if I left him, he said he would kill me.

Prostitution is a dangerous lifestyle, and some guys will rape, rob, and kill you. I had friends missing after a date. Did the date kill her? Or had she managed to use that data to get away from her pimp? Others had pimps worse than mine, and one by the name of Filmore Slim had a stable of many women. Rumor had it; one of his girls kept money back, he stabbed and raped her with a bottle. I'm not sure if these stories were meant to maintain your obedience to your man or if these things happened.

All I knew was when girls went missing; you didn't know if they were dead by drugs, pimps, or their tricks. Were they able to escape? It was a way of life and a horrible one at that.

I don't know what changed my mind, but I guess I preferred to die when I turned eighteen years old than to be with Bobby, and I escaped.

Many things in the next few years happened, but I want to keep this explanation of my life short.

Even though I got away from Bobby, I didn't know how to take care of myself. I only had a seventh-grade education during that day, and the only profession I learned was to be a hooker. I found jobs as a go-go dancer, or at other times, I was a stripper, which I felt was a step up.

Still, on a quest to find love, I married four times. I wanted an everyday life, but it was elusive. I'd been down a rabbit hole so young and had seen so much, which caused me many problems. It was like Humpty dumpty had taken a fall, and nothing I could do would put my life back together.

By now, I was taking drugs. Just pills in those days, but I became a speed freak, which was amphetamines. I had children, and because of my poor choices, I lost custody.

One of my past relationships was with a man named Frank. When we had a true confession, I told him about my past, and his confession was one of a pervert. He liked to look at women through the window and masturbate. His confession discussed me, but we had twins, and I focused on getting my life together and regaining custody of the children I lost.

Then one day, I went to the laundromat. I left Frank with the twins, who were eight months old. When I reached the laundromat, all the washers were in use. I didn't want to wait and returned home immediately. Walking in the door, I could hear here, my daughter crying. I found Frank using a baby pacifier on my daughter while jacking himself off.

I was outraged, and the only reason I didn't kill him was that I wasn't strong enough. Having murder in one's heart is frightening, and now give, thanks to God, I wasn't strong enough. Neither would I wish this anger on anyone!

By this time in my life, everyone seemed to fail me, and all my hopes and dreams were crushed. Broken, I had no more fight left in me. People I turned to seemed to dash all my aspirations of me putting my life back together and the chance of getting my other children returned. At which point, I became unable to cope and became an alcoholic.

Drunk, I realized I didn't want my life to influence my twins and decided to put them in foster care. Even though I didn't find someone to love me, I still loved them and wanted what was best for them.

Angry and mad at the world, I became an outlaw, which meant I didn't have a pimp. Returning to Guam, I went back into prostitution. Furious with what I had seen of men, I was angry. I wasn't a lesbian but had still lost all respect for the men in my generation.

I can't recall how much time had passed, but my daughter passed away while the twins were in foster care. A social worker came to the massage studio I was working at and told me she had run a fever, and it was too much for her heart. I felt she died of a broken heart, which broke my heart even more.

Then a day came, I heard that Jesus was supposed to return. Religion was not a part of my life, but I was amazed to listen to this story. How was he going to come back?

Then one-day early morning, I went to the base to get coffee. Back then, we didn't have cafes in the villages. I was standing at the gate, waiting for a base taxi to take me to a restaurant. Standing at the guard station, the guard spotted a UFO. It was early dawn, and there was no mistaking what it was. Silver, round and red flashing lights came on. You couldn't tell if a cloud moved or if it merged into the cloud, but this was how it disappeared from view.

It was also during those days a book had come out called chariot of the gods. And this was when I found out UFO's were mentioned in Scripture.

And it was then I headed to the store and bought every Bible written a Bible concordance and dictionary. Reading the Bible, I realized I was a fornicator even though I had to look that word up. I always thought of myself as a good person, as I never hurt anyone else on purpose. And like I said, a simple person, all I knew is I'd been in hell all my life, and I sure didn't want to end up in a worse place after I died.

Reading Scripture, I fell in love with Jesus and related to Mary Magdalene. And now, finally, I found someone who loved me.

And because I loved Christ back, I wanted to be the best person I could be.

Every evening, I would sit on the beach shore to pray and ask God via Jesus to save me as the Bible said to turn to him. Usually, I'd pray and ask what I should do. Close my eyes, open the Bible, and point. I'd read, "will there be any faith. I'd read, "you have to be perfect because God is perfect." Found in Matthew nineteen: twenty-one and Matthew five: forty-eight. Then when I read forsake all, pick up your cross and follow me. I, of course, quit my job and emptied my safe deposit box and gave everything away.

Reading Scripture, I understood Solomon had built a temple and asked the Lord if people turned to that temple, he would hear them. Not having a formal education, I had no clue the temple Solomon built was no longer there and decided I'd go to Israel to the temple.

Before leaving for Israel, a Bible in hand, and for reasons I can't explain, I walked out into the water to the reef where there is a tiny uninhabited island.

That day I spent on the seashore singing and praying the entire day. I felt I was waiting for something but didn't know why or what. It was turning dusk, and three men on a tiny rowboat appeared on the other side of a drop-off. The water was usually 1 to 3 feet deep except in this one section, which was no more than five feet across.

They said something about Tyre, and to this day, I can't tell you what they said. But when I answered them back, I told them I was not afraid. I immediately jumped into the drop-off and swam to the other side in three or four strokes, but when I got there, they were gone.

By this time, the only light available was the moonlight, and I could see moving shadows on the side of this tiny island. I assumed it was these three men, and instead, it was a huge rock.

And this is when it got strange. I have never lied and will list the Bible verses that I have trusted on this. First being, ***Behold ye among the heathen, and regard, and wonder***

marvellously: for I will work a work in your days, which ye will not believe, though it be told you Hab 1:5.

I ended getting up on this rock but spread eagle when there arose what seemed like the wind but not a breeze you could feel only hear. That wind went into me, and I know it is God's Spirit. I can actually sense and see like a light that comes out my eyes. Mt 16:13-20, Rom 6:5. Jn 3:8.

The rock the size of an automobile was no longer there some days later.

In any case, after this happened, I moved to this tiny island for two years. Dedicating my life to God and celibacy Richard, an ex-boyfriend witnessed my change, and he brought food and supplies out every week.

The two years I lived on this tiny island, I did nothing but study the Bible. This was when I started to learn what I have written in this book.

After which I traveled to many places in this world. Sure I took some missteps and faltered along the way. I was just a person no one believed.

Eventually, I made it to Israel and found out Solomons temple was not there, but in the meantime, I believe I found his wisdom.

God promised we would have many children. I failed in this world as a mother, but know I won't go wrong with God's help when it comes to the new world. And believe with all my heart one day I will have many children.

Printed in the United States
By Bookmasters